THE DECADES OF TWENTIETH-CENTURY AMERICA

AMERICA IN THE 1960s

EDMUND LINDOP with
MARGARET J. GOLDSTEIN

Twenty-First Century Books · Minneapolis

Twenty-First Century Books
A division of Lerner Publishing Group, Inc.
241 First Avenue North
Minneapolis, MN 55401 U.S.A.

Website address: www.lernerbooks.com

Library of Congress Cataloging-in-Publication Data

Lindop, Edmund.
    America in the 1960s / by Edmund Lindop with Margaret J. Goldstein.
        p.   cm. — (The decades of twentieth-century America)
    Includes bibliographical references and index.
    ISBN 978-0-7613-3453-8 (lib. bdg. : alk. paper)
    1. United States—History—1961–1969—Juvenile literature.
    2. Nineteen sixties—Juvenile literature. I. Goldstein, Margaret J.
    II. Title. III. Title: America in the nineteen sixties.
    E841.L56 2010
        973.923—dc22   2007038028

Manufactured in the United States of America
1 2 3 4 5 6 – PA – 15 14 13 12 11 10

CONTENTS ★★★★★★★★★★★★★★★★★★★

PROLOGUE   5

FROM **OLD TO NEW**

CHAPTER ONE   11

INTO THE **FIRE:** U.S. Foreign Policy

CHAPTER TWO   29

HOME **FRONT:** The Civil Rights Fight

CHAPTER THREE   45

"ONE GIANT LEAP FOR MANKIND":
Science and Technology in the 1960s

CHAPTER FOUR   55

THE GREAT **SOCIETY:**
The 1960s Economy

CHAPTER FIVE   59

LIBERATION! Social Change in the 1960s

CHAPTER SIX   69

VOICES: Writing of the 1960s

CHAPTER SEVEN   81

POP! Art and Design of the 1960s

CHAPTER EIGHT   93

STAGE**CRAFT:**
Stage and Screen in the 1960s

CHAPTER NINE   105

"MY GENERATION": Music in the 1960s

CHAPTER TEN   117

"THE THRILL OF VICTORY":
Sports in the 1960s

EPILOGUE   129

FOREVER **AFTER**

★★★★★★★★★★★★★★★★★★★

TIMELINE   132

SOURCE NOTES   134

SELECTED BIBLIOGRAPHY   135

TO LEARN MORE   137

SELECTED 1960s CLASSICS   139

1960s ACTIVITY   140

INDEX   141

PRESIDENT-ELECT JOHN F. KENNEDY *(right)* shakes hands
with President Dwight D. Eisenhower in December 1960.

FROM OLD TO NEW

When he left office in 1961, President Dwight D. Eisenhower was seventy years old. At that time, he was the oldest man ever to serve as president of the United States. Eisenhower was a plain-talking military man. He had grown up in Kansas, in a hardworking family without much money. He had led the Allied military forces in Europe during World War II (1939–1945) and had led the United States as president through most of the 1950s. Americans of the 1950s looked at Eisenhower as a kind of father figure: wise, steady, and a bit old-fashioned. His wife, Mamie, was equally ordinary and old-fashioned. As First Lady, she avoided the spotlight.

In contrast, John F. Kennedy was forty-three years old when he took office in 1961. He was the youngest man ever elected to the office of president. Kennedy was handsome and stylish. He had grown up in a wealthy family in Boston, Massachusetts. He was friendly with socialites and Hollywood stars. His wife, Jacqueline (Jackie), was glamorous and beautiful. With two small children and bold new ideas for the United States, John F. Kennedy was all about the future.

When the Eisenhowers vacated the White House to make way for the incoming Kennedys, the contrast could not have been clearer. The oldest U.S. president handed off the torch of leadership to the youngest U.S. president.

5

Eisenhower represented the old era: the staid and conservative 1950s. Kennedy represented the new era: the youthful, rebellious 1960s.

■ SUPERPOWER

Most Americans were optimistic in the 1950s. The United States had emerged from World War II as the wealthiest and most powerful nation on Earth. Soldiers returning from the war enrolled in college, got married, and bought houses. Factories churned out consumer goods such as televisions, refrigerators, and big flashy cars. The U.S. economy boomed. New highways, new housing developments, and new businesses—everything seemed new in the 1950s. There were lots of new kids too. Young couples were having babies—so many, in fact, that sociologists made up a name for the exploding U.S. population: the baby boom. To care for their children, most white, middle-class mothers stayed home and did housework.

But despite all the new houses, cars, and kids, the 1950s was not without its problems. For one thing, the United States wasn't the only "superpower" to emerge after World War II. The Soviet Union (a union of fifteen republics including Russia) had also become big, strong, and powerful. This former U.S. ally was a Communist nation. That meant the government there controlled all business and property. The government also told people where to work and where to live. Soviet citizens couldn't even vote for their own leaders.

In the United States—a capitalist democracy—people are free to run their own businesses, own their own homes, elect their own leaders, and

A STEREOTYPICAL 1950S SCENE includes many children playing on broad suburban streets.

make their own decisions. Most Americans thought Communism was a terrible form of government. After World War II, the Soviet Union had conquered and then forced its Communist system onto nations in Eastern Europe. Americans began to worry that the Soviet Union would take over even more countries—and perhaps even attack the United States.

To defend itself against the Soviet threat, the U.S. government stockpiled guns, tanks, and missiles. It stocked up on deadly nuclear bombs, which it tested over Nevada, the Pacific Ocean, and other sparsely populated places. The U.S. government also tried to root out any Communists who might be living in the United States. Urged on by Senator Joseph McCarthy of Wisconsin, government agents investigated Americans with alleged Communist leanings. Many suspected Communists were blacklisted, meaning employers wouldn't hire them.

While the United States built up its military supplies, the Soviet Union did so too. This military buildup was called an arms race. The two nations also engaged in a space race:

The Soviets launched **SPUTNIK 1** in 1957.

each rushed to be first to launch a spacecraft into outer space. Americans fumed when the Soviets scored the first victory in the space race, launching *Sputnik 1* into orbit in October 1957.

The tensions between the United States and the Soviet Union came to be called the Cold War (1945–1991). The two nations didn't fight directly during the Cold War. Instead, the Soviet Union helped other Communist countries, and the United States helped countries that were fighting Communism. For example, in Southeast Asia in 1957, Communist North Vietnam went to war with non-Communist South Vietnam. The United States sent money and military advisers to help the South Vietnamese. The Soviet Union and China, another big Communist country, sent help to North Vietnam.

■ THE OTHER AMERICANS

Back at home, not everyone in the United States was living the good life. Many African Americans were poor in the 1950s. Employers gave them the lowest-paying jobs: housecleaner, shoe shiner, and farmhand. While white Americans were enjoying the latest in household electronics, some black households didn't have electricity or telephones. Many African Americans didn't have enough food to eat.

In addition to poverty, many black Americans endured segregation—the enforced separation of blacks and whites in public places. In the South, black children were not allowed to attend school with whites. African Americans

In the southern United States, **PUBLIC FACILITIES WERE SEGREGATED,** with separate areas for whites and for African Americans.

could not eat at restaurants with whites, attend the same colleges, drink from the same water fountains, or use the same restrooms. On city buses, whites sat in the front and blacks sat in the back. If the white section was full, blacks in the back had to stand and give up their seats to white riders. Few blacks voted in the South in the 1950s because government officials wouldn't allow them to register. Often these restrictions were written into the law. White Americans also enforced the regulations using terror: they threatened, beat, and killed African Americans who challenged white supremacy.

Black leaders led the fight for change. They wanted to end segregation. They also wanted equal opportunities in education, housing, voting, and employment. Using boycotts, court cases, and peaceful protest marches, black Americans made small but groundbreaking gains in the 1950s. The Reverend Martin Luther King Jr. emerged as the leader of the civil rights (equal rights) movement.

■ "LET THE GOOD TIMES ROLL"

Despite the political and social tensions, Americans had lots of fun in the 1950s. Rock-and-roll music arrived with Elvis Presley. Television programs such as *I Love Lucy* and *Your Show of Shows* kept audiences in stitches. Some people loved big-league baseball. Others adored the movies.

Most Americans were patriotic. They didn't trust Communists, but they trusted their leaders to protect them—with nuclear weapons if necessary. Outside of civil rights marchers, few Americans protested during the 1950s. Sure, there were a few who did—artists, writers, and "beatniks" who gathered in the coffeehouses of New York and San Francisco. But they were a tiny minority. For the most part, Americans were conformist and comfortable in the 1950s. Few people suspected that beneath the nation's squeaky-clean veneer, a volcano was waiting to erupt.

ELVIS PRESLEY ushered in the era of rock-and-roll music in the 1950s.

"I was sixteen years old and I believed it. I really believed that I was going to be able to change the world."

—*Peace Corps volunteer, 1961*

THE FIRST PEACE CORPS VOLUNTEERS board a plane for overseas duty on August 29, 1961. They served in Ghana, Africa.

CHAPTER ONE

INTO THE FIRE:
U.S. FOREIGN POLICY

Newly elected president John F. Kennedy had big plans for the United States. He challenged Americans—especially young people—to think big. "The torch has been passed to a new generation of Americans," Kennedy said at his inaugural address on January 20, 1961. Then he uttered his most famous line, "Ask not what your country can do for you. Ask what you can do for your country."

On the heels of this challenge, Kennedy introduced an exciting new program. In March 1961, he created the Peace Corps. The word *corps* usually refers to a military unit. But the Peace Corps was not a fighting force. Kennedy's plan was to send volunteers to foreign nations to help poor people. The volunteers would set up schools, health clinics, and irrigation systems. They would teach farmers new techniques and help people organize small businesses. They would help end poverty and help make the world a more peaceful place.

The response to the idea was overwhelming. Within an hour after Kennedy announced the program, phone calls began flooding in to U.S. government offices. Thousands of young people wanted to join. "The whole idea was that you can make a difference," recalled one Peace Corps volunteer. "I was sixteen years old and I believed it. I really believed that I was going to be able to change the world." Another volunteer explained, "I'd never done anything political, patriotic, or unselfish, because nobody ever asked me to. Kennedy asked."

■ COMMUNISTS AT THE DOORSTEP

While Peace Corps volunteers trained for service in Africa, Asia, and other far-off lands, trouble was brewing for President Kennedy closer to home. Cuba, just 90 miles (145 kilometers) south of Florida in the Caribbean Sea, was a Communist nation. It had close ties to the Soviet Union. Its ruler, Fidel Castro, spewed angry words against the United States. Castro's government had seized U.S.-owned businesses and property in Cuba. Relations between the two nations grew tense.

The U.S. government devised a plan: A force of about fifteen hundred Cuban exiles—Cubans who had fled to the United States during Castro's Communist takeover of Cuba in 1959—would invade the island nation by sea. When they arrived, the Cuban people would immediately rise up and overthrow Castro's government. U.S. forces would back up the invaders with airpower.

That was the plan. The reality was much different: Cuba's intelligence agency learned about the invasion ahead of time. Meanwhile, U.S. officials couldn't agree on the best way to carry out the attack. They bickered and changed plans at the last minute. On

The United States and the Soviet Union appeared to be on the brink of nuclear war.

April 17, 1961, when the exiles came ashore at the Bay of Pigs in Cuba, Castro's forces quickly rushed in. U.S. air support came too little and too late to help the invaders. The Cuban defenders killed more than one hundred exiles and captured almost twelve hundred. The invasion was an embarrassment for President Kennedy. Meanwhile, Fidel Castro bragged about his victory over the mighty United States.

The Bay of Pigs invasion was just a warm-up to the next showdown in Cuba. To help protect its Communist ally, the Soviet Union secretly shipped tanks, airplanes, and other weapons to Cuba in 1962. It built missile-launching sites there, with nuclear missiles readied to attack the United States. U.S. spy planes discovered the missile sites on October 14, 1962. A few days later, President Kennedy demanded that the Soviets remove the missiles. He also ordered a naval blockade to keep additional Soviet arms shipments from reaching Cuba.

The United States and the Soviet Union appeared to be on the brink of nuclear war. The U.S. military readied its forces. But instead of fighting, over a few tense days, President Kennedy and Soviet leader Nikita Khrush-chev worked out a peace deal. The United States promised not to invade Cuba, and the Soviet Union agreed to remove its missiles from Cuba. In addition, the United States secretly agreed to remove its own nuclear weapons from Turkey, a nation near the Soviet Union.

With the crisis ended, Americans breathed a sigh of relief. President Kennedy's cool head during the crisis earned him great praise. The Cuban Missile Crisis also marked a turning point in the Cold War. In June 1963, the United States and the Soviet Union set up a direct telephone hotline between the White House and the Kremlin—the Soviet government offices. The phone line was designed to assist in future talks between the two superpowers.

Although many Americans continued to rail against Communists, 1963 marked a softening in U.S.–Soviet relations. People in both nations were starting to realize, in the words of President Kennedy, that "we all inhabit this small planet. We all breathe the same air. We all cherish our children's future. And we are all mortal."

The **BAY OF PIGS** invasion of 1961 was a military and political disaster. Here **JOHN F. KENNEDY** *(second from left)* meets with veterans of the doomed operation.

▉ THE END OF THE BEGINNING

The hope and optimism of John F. Kennedy's administration came crashing down on November 22, 1963. On that day, Kennedy was in Dallas, Texas, for political meetings and appearances. At about twelve thirty in the afternoon, he and Jackie rode in a motorcade through the streets of Dallas. They sat in the backseat of an open-topped limousine. Texas governor John Connally and his wife, Nellie, sat in the front seat.

As the Kennedys smiled and waved to the cheering crowds, Nellie Connally turned to speak to John Kennedy. "Mr. President," she said, "you certainly can't say that Dallas doesn't love you!" No sooner were the words out of her mouth when gunshots rang out. The first bullet hit Kennedy in the neck. The next hit Governor Connally in the back. A third shot blew off part of Kennedy's head.

The scene turned to chaos. The crowds stopped cheering and began to run and scream. Secret Service agents rushed to the president's car. The limousine raced to a nearby hospital.

John Connally survived his wounds, but John Kennedy died at the hospital at about one in the afternoon. He was forty-six years old. On the plane carrying Kennedy's body back to Washington, D.C., Vice President Lyndon Baines Johnson took the oath of office as the new president of the United States. Later that afternoon, police arrested and charged Lee Harvey Oswald as the assassin.

JOHN F. KENNEDY AND HIS WIFE, JACKIE, ride with John and Nellie Connally *(bottom left and bottom center)* through downtown Dallas, Texas, on November 22, 1963.

A solemn **LYNDON B. JOHNSON** takes the oath of office aboard Air Force One (the presidential aircraft) shortly after John F. Kennedy's assassination on November 22, 1963.

Americans learned the news of Kennedy's death via radio, television, and word of mouth. Most were devastated. "I remember my 3rd grade teacher, Mrs. Burgess, started to cry, after the news was announced over the PA [public announcement] system," one woman recalled. "She then wrote 'President Lyndon Johnson' on the board and told the class that was our new president."

■ ROLLING THUNDER

With a heavy heart, Lyndon Johnson took over the presidency and the work that John F. Kennedy had begun. Before his death, Kennedy had pushed for passage of a civil rights act, which would outlaw discrimination in employment, voting, and public places. Johnson used skillful political pressure to ensure that Congress passed the act. He followed that early success with creation of new programs to fight poverty. Johnson's popularity rose quickly. He ran for president against Republican Barry Goldwater in 1964. Johnson won by a landslide.

Overseas, the Cold War still simmered. One hot spot was Vietnam, where Communist North Vietnam was still fighting non-Communist South Vietnam. Since the late 1950s, the United States had been sending money and military advisers to help the South Vietnamese. Gradually, the number of U.S. military personnel in Vietnam increased. These forces did not fight on the ground. Instead, they did such work as training South Vietnamese troops, intelligence gathering, and air reconnaissance, or observing enemy positions from airplanes. By late 1963, about 16,500 Americans were stationed in Vietnam.

The South Vietnamese government was corrupt and unstable. Military generals overthrew the South Vietnamese president in November 1963. The result was political chaos, with additional government takeovers soon after. The North Vietnamese took advantage of the chaos to increase their attacks in South Vietnam.

President Johnson was determined to bring stability to Vietnam. For one thing, he and his advisers did not want to see South Vietnam fall to Communists. But Johnson was also frustrated. The Communist successes made the United States look weak and ineffective. Johnson wanted to send ground troops to Vietnam. He believed that if the United States committed enough troops, it could easily defeat the Communists.

Johnson geared up for war. He convinced Congress to pass the Tonkin Gulf Resolution, authorizing him to conduct full-scale war in Vietnam. Meanwhile, the North Vietnamese made more inroads in South Vietnam. In February 1965, they attacked a

U.S. military base at Pleiku. The attack killed eight Americans and wounded more than one hundred.

President Johnson ordered retaliation. He begin Operation Rolling Thunder—the bombing of industrial

President Johnson was determined to bring stability to Vietnam. . . . He believed that if the United States committed enough troops, it could easily defeat the Communists.

and military targets in North Vietnam. He also sent the first ground forces to Vietnam. On March 8, 1965, the Ninth Marine Expeditionary Brigade came ashore at Da Nang, South Vietnam. For the United States, the Vietnam War had officially begun. By March 1966, approximately 215,000 Americans were fighting in Vietnam.

■ SEARCH AND DESTROY

The Vietnam War was unlike other wars the United States had fought. In World War II, for instance, armies had invaded and defended big chunks of territory. The front lines—where

U.S. soldiers battle guerrillas in the jungles of South Vietnam during the **VIETNAM WAR**.

opposing armies met one another—were well defined.

That was not the case in Vietnam. In addition to conventional forces, the North Vietnamese teamed up with guerrilla fighters called Vietcong. The guerrillas worked in small teams—sometimes even alone. They hid in the thick jungles of Vietnam, waiting for U.S. troops. They attacked by surprise and then disappeared back into the forest. Vietcong snipers, or lone sharpshooters, sometimes picked off U.S. soldiers one by one.

To fight the guerrillas, the United States also used small groups of soldiers—squads of twelve men or less. Helicopters ferried the squads from base camps into the jungle. There, using a tactic called search and destroy, U.S. troops tried to root out guerrillas with guns and grenades. One U.S. Marine recalled the horrors—not only of fighting an unseen enemy but also coping with the leeches, bugs, and razor-sharp grasses that filled Vietnamese jungles:

> We had maybe five or six people to a squad, and a full marine squad is twelve people. We had been chewed up in the ambush. . . . Booby traps, snipers, heat exhaustion, disease. . . . Our feet were wet all the time. . . . Even if it wasn't the rainy season, that jungle was still dripping water on you. And if you were in an open area where it was

hot, you were wading through rivers or [rice] paddies or something. Constantly wet.

It seemed like the whole country was an enemy. The animals, the reptiles, the insects, the plants. . . . You get these ungodly cuts all over your hands and arms from the vegetation. . . . The cuts get infected. They turn into big open sores. . . . I've got scars all up and down my legs from leech bites.

After days without seeing the enemy, Americans often found themselves in sudden, bloody firefights. U.S. casualties quickly mounted. In 1965 about fourteen hundred U.S. troops lost their lives in Vietnam. In 1966 the number jumped to five thousand.

U.S. troops wade through waters of the **MEKONG RIVER IN THE SOUTHERN PART OF SOUTH VIETNAM** in April 1967.

U.S Air Force planes drop **AGENT ORANGE** over a Vietcong stronghold in South Vietnam.

■ HEY, HEY, LBJ!

As the war in Vietnam escalated, Americans began to ask questions. First of all, Where in the world *was* Vietnam? Many Americans had never even heard of the place. After that people wanted to know: Why was the United States trying to prop up the corrupt South Vietnamese government? But most of all, people asked: Why were so many young Americans dying in Vietnam?

It seemed to many that the war in Vietnam was unjust. It was also a waste of lives. Not only were thousands of young Americans dying, U.S. bombs were also killing civilians in North Vietnam. And U.S. soldiers often couldn't distinguish between guerrilla fighters and ordinary civilians. As a result, U.S. troops sometimes killed innocent Vietnamese—even women and children. In the quest to root out guerrillas, U.S. soldiers sometimes set fire to whole villages.

The United States used new, ghastly weapons in Vietnam. It used napalm bombs to set fire to enemy installations. But napalm—a kind of jelled gasoline—also splattered over a wide area, sometimes hitting civilians and burning them severely. U.S. forces used a chemical called Agent Orange to kill crops, thereby destroying enemy food supplies, and to strip leaves off branches, thus exposing enemy positions in the jungle. But Agent Orange also made people sick with cancer and skin diseases.

The more Americans learned about Vietnam, the angrier they became. They began to protest the war at rallies and "teach-ins." Most antiwar activity took place on college campuses. In the 1950s, most college students had been conformist and complacent. But times had changed. Inspired by the work of civil rights activists, young people knew that they, too, could protest to bring about change. They put their energy to work to end the Vietnam War.

19

For college-age men, the war in Vietnam posed personal as well as political problems. In July 1965, President Johnson announced that he was doubling the draft (call to military service). Instead of seventeen thousand men each month, the government would call up thirty-five thousand men for military service (very few women served in the military during the Vietnam War and only as volunteers). Some young men volunteered to serve in Vietnam. They felt it was their duty as U.S. citizens. But other young men wanted no part of the war, which they believed to be unjust and illegal. Nor did they want to die a gruesome death in the jungles of Vietnam. College students could get a student deferment—an exemption from the draft. But once they graduated, they were likely to be drafted.

Young men began to actively resist the draft. Some left the United States to live in Canada. Others refused to be inducted (drafted)—even choosing jail sentences over service in Vietnam. Still others became conscientious objectors, refusing to bear arms for religious or philosophical reasons. Many young men burned their draft cards in symbolic protest of the war.

The typical draft resister was white, well-off, and college educated. Poor young men, especially blacks and Hispanics, were less likely to have access to student deferments, legal assistance, and other draft-avoidance methods. As a result, U.S. forces in Vietnam were disproportionately black, brown, and poor.

■ DOVES AND HAWKS

In October 1967, after months of organizing, more than one hundred thousand antiwar protesters rallied in Washington, D.C. The demonstrators waved signs, listened to speeches, and sang protest songs. They chanted antiwar slogans such as "Hey, hey, LBJ [Lyndon Baines Johnson], how many kids did you kill today?" At one point, at the Pentagon (U.S. military headquarters near Washington, D.C.), soldiers roughed up some of the demonstrators. They even hit some marchers with billy clubs.

Young men burn their **DRAFT CARDS.**

Many Americans believed the Vietnam War was unjust and immoral. Many attended antiwar protests. But few Americans were willing to risk imprisonment for their antiwar beliefs. Two brothers, Daniel and Philip Berrigan, were among the exceptions. Both went to prison—several times—for their antiwar activities. The Berrigan brothers were born in Minnesota. As young men, both became Catholic priests. Both brothers were also pacifists—people who oppose war on moral and religious grounds. In the early 1960s, they became active in the civil rights movement. Then they joined the antiwar movement.

Philip Berrigan, the elder of the two brothers, was the first to take direct action against the Vietnam War. In October 1967, he and three other men walked into a Selective Service office in Baltimore, Maryland. As astonished employees looked on, the Baltimore Four, as they were later called, poured blood onto draft records in file cabinets. Some of the blood was Philip Berrigan's own. In a statement to the press, Berrigan explained, "We shed our blood willingly and gratefully. . . . We pour it upon these files to illustrate that with them and with these offices begins the pitiful waste of American and Vietnamese blood ten thousand miles [16,000 km] away." Seven months later, Daniel Berrigan joined his brother and seven others in

PHILIP BERRIGAN *(LEFT)* AND HIS BROTHER DANIEL BERRIGAN helped burn two baskets of draft board records in Catonsville, Maryland.

a similar protest. This time, at a Selective Service office in Catonsville, Maryland, the activists—later called the Catonsville Nine—gathered about six hundred files of young American men eligible for the draft. They took the files out into the parking lot and burned them with homemade napalm. After the Vietnam War ended, the Berrigan brothers joined the antinuclear movement. Philip Berrigan died in 2002. Daniel Berrigan remains active in the fight for peace and social justice.

21

Yet many Americans supported the Vietnam War. They believed it was a just and noble cause. The killing in Vietnam seemed to be part of the cost of war. But the sight of rebellious young people in the nation's capital bothered them a great deal. The protesters insulted the president and the nation. Some even shouted obscenities. Others wore raggedy clothing, long hair, and beards—the costume of the new "hippie" movement that was then sweeping the nation. Conservative Americans saw the protesters as disrespectful and unpatriotic.

Some Americans believed that Communists were the driving force behind the antiwar protests. Communists or not, the U.S. government was determined to shut down the antiwar movement. To disrupt further agitation, the Federal Bureau of Investigation (FBI) spied on antiwar leaders and organizations. For a time, the Selective Service System, the government agency in charge of the draft, targeted war protesters specifically. Selective Service removed some protesters' deferments and sent them to Vietnam.

■ BLOOD RED, WHITE, AND BLUE

By late 1967, the United States was in crisis over the Vietnam War. With billions of dollars spent and thousands of lives lost in the war, the public

ANTIWAR DEMONSTRATORS gather around the Washington Monument in Washington, D.C., on October 21, 1967.

was distressed and divided. President Johnson and his staff tried to salvage public support for the war. General William Westmoreland, the head of U.S. forces in Vietnam, told reporters that the United States had the upper hand in the fighting. U.S. troops were making progress, he said, and would be able to withdraw in less than two years.

But Americans learned otherwise during the Tet Offensive of January and February 1968. During more than three weeks of fighting, the Vietcong launched bloody attacks on the cities of South Vietnam. Although U.S. troops eventually drove back the enemy, the offensive made it clear that the Vietcong were nowhere near defeated.

Meanwhile, the presidential primaries had begun. Several antiwar candidates entered the race on the Democratic side. One was Eugene McCarthy, a liberal senator from Minnesota. Another was Robert F. Kennedy, a senator from New York and younger brother of slain president John F. Kennedy. In addition to opposing the war, Kennedy was a tireless campaigner for the poor and for minorities. Many young voters jumped on the McCarthy and Kennedy bandwagons.

Then the bloodshed came home. First, in April, civil rights leader Martin Luther King Jr. fell to an assassin's bullet. In addition to his civil rights

Tet is the start of the Vietnamese New Year. It lasts for seven days in winter. During the early years of the Vietnam War, all fighting stopped during Tet. Instead, both North Vietnamese and South Vietnamese celebrated the New Year. But in 1968, instead of a cease-fire, the North Vietnamese attacked during the Tet holiday. The attacks came mainly in South Vietnamese cities. They caught U.S. troops and their South Vietnamese allies by complete surprise. The worst violence occurred in Saigon, the South Vietnamese capital, and in the old capital city of Hue. The bloodshed was horrific. Across South Vietnam, more than 14,300 civilians died in the fighting. Hundreds of thousands lost their homes. Eventually, U.S. and South Vietnamese forces took back control in South Vietnamese cities. But the Tet Offensive had far-ranging effects. Most important, it showed Americans that the North Vietnamese were nowhere near defeated. Afterward, U.S. TV news announcer Walter Cronkite proclaimed that the United States was "mired in stalemate" in Vietnam. "The only rational way out then," he said, "will be to negotiate, not as victors but as an honorable people who lived up to their pledge to defend democracy, and did the best they could." The lessons of the Tet Offensive helped swell the ranks of the antiwar movement. On March 12, 1968, antiwar candidate Eugene McCarthy won an astounding 42 percent of the vote in the New Hampshire Democratic primary. Robert Kennedy jumped into the presidential race four days later. President Johnson, meanwhile, changed his stance on Vietnam. He announced that he would reduce the bombing of North Vietnam, deny General Westmoreland's request for two hundred thousand more troops, and seek out peace negotiations with the North Vietnamese. And in a move that surprised the public, Johnson also told Americans, "I shall not seek, and I will not accept, the nomination of my party for another term as your president."

struggles, King had become an outspoken opponent of the war in Vietnam. His death saddened and shocked the nation, especially African Americans. Two months later, an assassin killed Robert Kennedy on the campaign trail in Los Angeles, California. Once again, Americans were crushed.

Disillusioned with the political system, antiwar activists took to the streets. They staged a big peace demonstration at the Democratic National Convention in Chicago, Illinois, that summer. Outside the convention hall, the scene turned ugly as police and the National Guard attacked the demonstrators with tear gas and billy clubs. Inside, the Democrats chose Vice President Hubert Humphrey as their presidential nominee.

■ RIGHT FACE

The Republicans, meanwhile, nominated Richard Nixon as their presidential candidate. Nixon had had a long career in politics. He had served many years in Congress and had served as U.S. vice president under Dwight D. Eisenhower. He had narrowly lost the 1960 presidential election to John F. Kennedy.

Nixon was a conservative. He knew that many Americans were shocked by the changes taking place in U.S. society—young people demonstrating in the streets, refusing to serve in the military, and growing their hair long. In addition, black Americans, frustrated by poverty and police brutality, had recently rioted in many U.S. inner cities. These riots, too, shocked mainstream voters.

Police attempt to disperse **ANTIWAR PROTESTERS** at the 1968 Democratic National Convention in Chicago, Illinois.

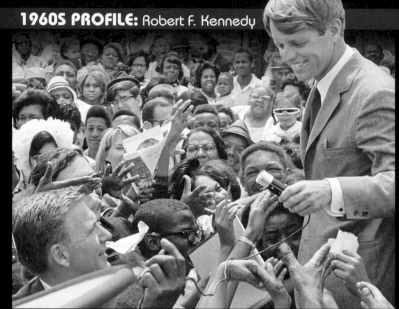

SENATOR ROBERT KENNEDY greets a crowd of supporters in Indiana during his race for the Democratic presidential nomination in 1968.

When people think of the 1960s, they often think of John F. Kennedy. But John's brother Robert F. Kennedy (RFK) was just as popular. Bobby, as Robert was often called, was the seventh of nine Kennedy children. Their father was a millionaire banker and diplomat from Boston, Massachusetts. Trained as a lawyer, Bobby entered politics in 1952, when he managed John's campaign for the U.S. Senate. In 1960 Bobby again managed John's campaign—this time helping his brother win the presidency. John appointed Bobby to his cabinet, as attorney general of the United States. In this job, RFK oversaw the conviction of many organized crime figures. He also enforced civil rights laws. During the Cuban Missile Crisis, RFK played a key role in the decision to negotiate with the Soviets rather than resort to war. After John's assassination,

Robert Kennedy became a senator from New York. He also awakened to the plight of the nation's poor. He visited inner cities, the rural South, and migrant labor camps. In the Senate, Kennedy promoted programs to help poor Americans. As the Vietnam War heated up, he added his voice to the antiwar movement. In March 1968, he entered the presidential race. After winning a number of key primaries, he seemed poised to win the Democratic nomination. Then, on June 5, a Jordanian immigrant named Sirhan Sirhan shot and killed Kennedy in Los Angeles. Once again, the nation mourned the loss of a great leader. "RFK was going to restore the magic and vision [of his brother]," one woman remembered. "He was going to relight the torch." Tragically, another Kennedy's torch had been extinguished far too soon.

Republican candidate Richard Nixon *(left)*, with his wife, Pat, drives down Chestnut Street in Philadelphia, Pennsylvania, in September 1968. A banner reading **"NIXON'S THE ONE"** is stretched across the street.

Nixon appealed to these voters, the "forgotten Americans," as he called them, "those who did not indulge in violence, those who did not break the law, people who pay their taxes and go to work, people who send their children to school, who go to their churches, people who are not haters, people who love their country." Nixon also had a name for the antiwar protesters. He called them bums. In a three-way race between Nixon, Humphrey, and former Alabama governor George Wallace, a segregationist, the voters chose Nixon.

On the campaign trail, Richard Nixon had claimed to have a "secret plan" to end the Vietnam War. In fact, he had no plan. Early in his term, Nixon even escalated the war by secretly bombing Communist bases in Cambodia, a nation adjacent to Vietnam—thereby extending the war into another country. Meanwhile, Nixon announced that he would bring some U.S. troops home from Vietnam—arguing that the South Vietnamese needed to take over the fight for themselves.

In June 1969, U.S. troop strength peaked at 543,000 Americans in Vietnam. By then almost 35,000 Americans had died in the war. Antiwar protests continued. The largest ever, the Moratorium to End the War in Vietnam, took place in Washington, D.C., in October. The crowd of demonstrators numbered at least 600,000. President Nixon continued to insult the antiwar protesters. He watched a college football game on television during the moratorium. But even Nixon acknowledged that, somehow, the United States needed to get out of Vietnam.

27

These four students at a Greensboro, North Carolina, lunch counter launched the
SUCCESSFUL CIVIL RIGHTS "SIT-IN" MOVEMENT OF THE 1960S.

CHAPTER TWO

HOME FRONT:
THE CIVIL RIGHTS FIGHT

On February 1, 1960, four black male students from North Carolina Agricultural and Technical College walked into a Woolworth variety store in Greensboro, North Carolina. They bought a few personal items and then sat down at the store's lunch counter. There was just one problem. The lunch counter was segregated. That meant that only whites could eat there. "I'm sorry," the waitress told the four young men, "we don't serve Negroes here."

The four students already knew the lunch counter would deny them service. That's why they sat at the counter—to force the issue, to bring attention to the injustice of segregation, and to demand change. Refusing to leave, the four young men sat at the counter for another hour, until the store closed for the day. The next day, they sat at the counter again—and about twenty more African American students joined them. On the third day, more students crowded the counter, this time whites as well as blacks. Soon the counter was overflowing with protesters. The "sit-in" movement spread—to more segregated lunch counters in Greensboro and to other lunch counters across the South.

As the movement grew, tension mounted. Crowds of angry whites heckled and taunted protesters at the sit-ins. Some whites dumped sugar, ketchup, and mustard

on the protesters' heads. But still the students sat. They did not fight back. The civil rights movement by then had become well organized. Civil rights leader Martin Luther King Jr. taught the principle of nonviolence. Peaceful but relentless protest was more effective than violent action, he explained.

Like a swelling wave, the civil rights movement grew larger. Throughout the winter of 1960, African Americans and small numbers of white supporters staged sit-ins, marches, and boycotts against segregated businesses in the South. Sometimes, police officers arrested the protesters. Other times, officers beat the protesters, or they stood by and allowed angry white mobs to do the beating.

But the protests continued—with results. Sit-ins were bad for business. Losing money, many stores chose to desegregate rather than face continued protests. On May 10, 1960, six Nashville, Tennessee, stores desegregated their lunch counters. In July the Greensboro lunch counters desegregated. By the end of 1960, hundreds of other stores had followed suit.

■ FREEDOM RIDES

After their victories at lunch counters, civil rights leaders turned to a new target—interstate bus stations. At most bus stations in the South, waiting rooms, restaurants, and restrooms were all segregated. Led by James Farmer, a group called the Congress of Racial Equality (CORE) decided to challenge this discrimination. Farmer devised the idea of "Freedom Rides." On these rides, groups of black and white protesters would travel by bus through the South. At bus stations along the way, blacks would use "white only" facilities and vice versa.

As before, the riders would remain nonviolent—no matter how much violence they faced. CORE instructed its activists:

> You may choose to face physical assault without protecting yourself, hands at the sides, unclenched; or you may choose to protect yourself, making plain you do not intend to hit back. . . . To protect the skull, fold the hands over the head. To prevent disfigurement of the face, bring the elbows together in front of the eyes. . . . To prevent internal injury from kicks, lie on the side and bring the knees upward to the chin.

"Fill up the jails . . . fill them to bursting if we have to."

—James Farmer, 1961

In addition to nonviolence, Freedom Riders pledged to use a tactic called "jail not bail." If arrested, they would go to jail rather than pay money (bail) to win their release. "Fill up the jails . . . fill them to bursting if we have to," Farmer exclaimed. The protesters knew that going to jail for their beliefs would win them many supporters. They also wanted to create hassles and extra costs for the authorities by forcing them to process and house large numbers of prisoners.

On May 4, 1961, thirteen CORE volunteers left Washington, D.C., by bus. They traveled first through Virginia, North Carolina, and Georgia, meeting little resistance at bus stations. En route to Alabama, the riders split into two groups, taking two different buses. In Anniston, Alabama, a crowd of angry whites attacked the first bus with clubs and iron bars. They slashed the bus's tires, smashed its windows, and tossed a firebomb through the door. The bus exploded into flames (all the passengers escaped unhurt).

31

DAZED FREEDOM RIDERS watch as their bus burns outside of Anniston, Alabama, in 1961.

> In his "Letter from Birmingham Jail," King explained that black Americans, who faced hatred, violence, poverty, segregation, and humiliation . . . were fed up with waiting.

The second bus traveled to Birmingham, Alabama. At the bus terminal, a mob savagely attacked the Freedom Riders with baseball bats and lead pipes. The police made no effort to help the riders. In fact, Birmingham police commissioner Bull Connor had deliberately kept his officers away from the terminal, so that the beating would take place without police interference.

The Freedom Rides continued and so did the violence. By then, though, the whole nation was watching on TV. The protests prompted the Kennedy administration to make changes. On November 1, 1961, a new federal law outlawed segregation in interstate bus facilities. The costs had been high, but the civil rights protesters had scored another victory.

■ BIRMINGHAM

In the early 1960s, Birmingham, Alabama, was one of the most segregated cities in the United States. Birmingham was also infamous for its vicious treatment of black citizens. Blacks who tried to organize or protest there risked beatings and bombings. In fact, Birmingham was nicknamed Bombingham after a series

of bombings in black neighborhoods between 1957 and 1963.

In the spring of 1963, Martin Luther King Jr. decided to confront segregation in Birmingham head-on. The confrontation was quick in coming. At sit-ins and marches, protesters found themselves face-to-face with Bull Connor's club-wielding police officers and ferocious police dogs.

Some protesters were bloodied. Others landed in jail. Martin Luther King Jr. was among the jailed marchers. From his prison cell, King wrote his famous "Letter from Birmingham Jail." The letter addressed those who cautioned that Birmingham wasn't ready for desegregation—those who told blacks to wait patiently for equal rights. King explained that black Americans, who faced hatred, violence, poverty, segregation, and humiliation on a daily basis, were fed up with waiting.

When King left jail a week later, he and other leaders saw the need for fresh recruits in the Birmingham protest movement. Many of the city's adults were unwilling to demonstrate. They feared going to jail and losing their jobs. To fill the void, King appealed to teenagers. Young people had less to lose and more energy for the fight. More than one thousand black Birmingham youngsters answered the call to join in civil rights protests in May.

Tragically, on May 3, Connor's officers turned police dogs and high-pressure water hoses on the young demonstrators. Like cannon blasts, jets of water knocked teenagers off their feet and left them bruised and bloodied. Police dogs did worse damage. Newspaper and television photographers caught the scene on film and delivered it to Americans' living rooms. The nation was horrified.

Meanwhile, the uproar in Birmingham hurt business in downtown shops. The city agreed to negotiate with King's team. The result was the desegregation of Birmingham's lunch counters, restrooms, drinking fountains, and other facilities; better job opportunities for African Americans in downtown stores; and other gains. Although resentment simmered on both sides, peace finally returned to Birmingham.

POLICE TURN HIGH-PRESSURE WATER HOSES on young African American protesters in Birmingham, Alabama, on May 3, 1963.

The biggest event of the civil rights movement—in terms of sheer numbers—was the 1963 March on Washington for Jobs and Freedom. At first, civil rights leaders worried that attendance would be low. But in towns and cities across the nation, African Americans organized "freedom buses" and "freedom trains" to get people to the nation's capital for the August 28 march. Some people even walked. In the end, more than 250,000 attended. Most of the marchers were black, but many whites joined the demonstration. Marchers carried signs that read "We March for Jobs for All Now," "We March for Integrated Schools Now," "We Demand Equal Rights Now," and similar slogans. Some world-famous folk musicians—Joan Baez; Peter, Paul, and Mary; and Odetta—led the crowd in song. Many people spoke that day, but the highlight was Martin Luther King Jr., who delivered his famous "I have a dream" speech. He spoke of a day in which racism and injustice would be eliminated from U.S. society. For rank-and-file marchers, the event was inspirational. "If I ever had any doubts [about fighting for civil rights] before, they're gone now," said Hazel Rivers, a marcher from Alabama. "I've followed it this far. When I get back there tomorrow I'm going to do whatever needs to be done—I don't care if it's picketing or marching or sitting-in or what, I'm ready to do it."

MARTIN LUTHER KING JR. delivers his "I have a dream" speech in Washington, D.C., on August 28, 1963.

■ SLOW, PAINFUL STEPS

Protests continued through 1963. The largest event was the massive March on Washington for Jobs and Freedom in August. In early 1964, a new civil rights bill made its way through Congress. The law forbade hotels, restaurants, theaters, and other facilities from excluding black customers. It outlawed

> **" Although you may be as white as a sheet,
> you will become as black as tar."**

—a black attorney speaking to a group of white Freedom Summer volunteers, 1964

racial discrimination by employers, labor unions, and other organizations. President Johnson signed the bill into law on July 2.

Along with this victory, civil rights leaders tackled voter registration. In southern states, local officials routinely kept blacks from registering. They used a number of tricks. They sometimes made black applicants take tests with complicated questions about state government. Test takers were sure to fail—the questions were so hard that not even lawyers would have known the answers. Other times, officials rejected black applicants if they made simple writing errors, such as failing to cross a *t* on a registration form.

But mostly, whites made sure that African Americans were too scared to register. For example, after Fannie Lou Hamer registered to vote in Mississippi, her employer, a white farmer, fired her and evicted her from his farm. Later, after Hamer tried to help other blacks register, the local police had her jailed and beaten.

It was into this atmosphere of fear and terror that idealistic college students came to Mississippi in the summer of 1964. Their project, Mississippi Freedom Summer, involved hundreds of volunteers, mostly white students from the North. They came to help black Mississippians register to vote and to open Freedom Schools, where volunteers would provide basic education to poor blacks.

Black leaders warned the students about the dangers they would face in Mississippi. "Although you may be as white as a sheet, you will become as black as tar," a black attorney cautioned a group of female volunteers. He explained that in Mississippi, white supremacists hated whites who helped blacks more than they hated blacks themselves.

On Sunday, June 21, three young civil rights workers—Andrew Goodman, a Mississippi Freedom Summer volunteer, and CORE workers James Chaney and Michael Schwerner—were expected back at CORE headquarters in Meridian, Mississippi, by evening. The three never arrived. When African Americans disappeared in Mississippi, the authorities rarely investigated.

But Goodman and Schwerner were white, and their disappearance made national headlines.

The FBI began a massive search for the three men. It eventually found their dead bodies buried at a farm outside Philadelphia, Mississippi. An investigation revealed that Philadelphia police had arrested the three for speeding—although speeding was just the excuse the officers had used to detain them. After Chaney paid a fine, the sheriff released the young men to a group of waiting Klansmen—members of the Ku Klux Klan, a violent white supremacist group. It was they who had murdered the young men with gunshots to the head.

After the tragedy, volunteers made considerable strides in registering voters and setting up Freedom Schools. They also established the Mississippi Freedom Democratic Party (MFDP), an alternative to the segregated Mississippi Democratic Party. The MFDP caused a procedural stir at the Democratic National Convention in August. In addition, MFDP delegate Fannie Lou Hamer told the convention about the brutal treatment she had received in Mississippi after registering to vote. Her speech reached a national television audience, including President Johnson. For Johnson and other U.S. leaders, civil rights and voting rights had become impossible to ignore.

In 1965 more blood was shed, this time in Alabama. There, Martin Luther King Jr. set out to lead a march from Selma to Montgomery, the state capital. The march was meant to protest police brutality and the denial of voting rights to blacks in Alabama. King warned the marchers that they might get beaten—and he was right. On the Edmund Pettus Bridge in Selma, state troopers attacked them with clubs, tear gas,

FANNY LOU HAMER speaks at the Democratic National Convention in Atlantic City, New Jersey, in 1964.

chains, charging horses, and cattle prods. The marchers never made it across the bridge, let alone to Montgomery. Once again, national television news showed the frantic scene to U.S. viewers.

Organizers would try again on March 21. But by then, President Johnson had intervened. He ordered almost twenty-five hundred army troops, the National Guard, FBI agents, and federal marshals to protect the marchers as they walked. Alabama governor George Wallace, a fierce segregationist, was seething with anger. But the thirty-two hundred marchers safely left Selma and covered the 54 miles (87 km) to Montgomery in five days. Along the way, they chanted and sang songs about freedom.

By then a voting rights act was working its way through Congress. This bill authorized federal officials to take over voter registration in places that discriminated against black voters. Although a few southern senators protested, the bill easily passed both the House and the Senate. President Johnson signed it on August 6, 1965.

■ "I'M BLACK AND I'M PROUD"

In the summer of 1966, a new voice entered the civil rights movement. He was Stokely Carmichael, newly elected head of the Student Nonviolent Coordinating Committee (SNCC), a student-led civil rights organization. Although Carmichael worked with Martin Luther King Jr. and other civil rights leaders to plan marches and sit-ins, his ideas were different. He was fed up with peaceful protest and patience. "The only way we're gonna stop them white men from whippin' us is to take over," Carmichael told a crowd in Greenwood, Mississippi. "We been saying freedom for six years—and we ain't got nothin'. What we gonna start now is 'Black Power.'" Quickly, the chant "Black Power, Black Power" arose from the crowd.

A new era in the fight for civil rights had begun. Previously, blacks had been careful and cautious. They always dressed conservatively during marches. They marched peacefully. They wanted to show themselves as responsible citizens who demanded equal treatment in U.S. society. They wanted to show that black families were no different from white families—with the same dreams for security, health, and happiness.

But Carmichael and his colleagues had a new approach. They felt that blacks sometimes had to resort to violence to confront the violence used against them. In addition, they didn't want to fit in with white society. They were proud to be black, proud of their African heritage, and proud to be different from whites. Some let their hair grow long, into big round Afros. Others studied African and African American history. In late 1966, SNCC expelled all whites from its organization. A few years later, soul singer James Brown recorded a song called "Say It Loud—I'm Black and I'm Proud."

Some African Americans took these ideas one step further. Huey Newton and Bobby Seale, two young black men from Oakland, California, formed the Black Panther Party for Self-Defense. The party was created to protect black Americans from police brutality. It also ran a number of social programs for poor blacks in Oakland. The Panthers called for violence—if necessary—to bring about justice for African Americans. Members dressed in military-style clothing and carried guns. They even talked of revolution—overthrow of the U.S. government. Gun-toting black activists and talk of revolution were alarming to U.S. authorities. The FBI inserted spies into the organization. Several members died in shootouts with the police.

BLACK PANTHERS stand outside a New York City courthouse under a quote from President Abraham Lincoln that reads "The Ultimate Justice of the People."

ike many black Americans, Malcolm Little learned about racism early in life. In 1931, when Malcolm was six, his father was found dead near a streetcar. The authorities ruled the death a suicide, but Malcolm's mother believed that white racists had killed her husband. In high school, Malcolm thought about studying to be a lawyer, but a teacher discouraged him. Blacks were not cut out to practice law, the teacher told him. After high school, Little turned to crime. He went to jail for burglary in 1946. In jail Little joined a group called the Nation of Islam, which preached that black people and white people should live separately. In 1952, after his release from prison, Little became a minister with the Nation of Islam. He also began calling himself Malcolm X. The *X*, he explained, represented the unknown names of African slaves in America.

MALCOLM LITTLE became Malcolm X after joining the Nation of Islam and becoming a minister.

Meanwhile, the civil rights movement was gaining strength in the United States. But Malcolm X didn't agree with civil rights leaders. He said that instead of meekly asking for equal rights, blacks should take political power in their own communities. He thought they should open their own businesses and secure their own economic freedom. He also thought that blacks might have to fight physically for equal rights. He scoffed at civil rights activists who peacefully sang "We Shall Overcome." "Today it's time to stop singing and start swinging [fists]," he told audiences. As Malcolm X became more and more defiant, he made many enemies. For one thing, the FBI didn't like his fiery rhetoric. It closely monitored his activities. He also made enemies within the Nation of Islam when he openly criticized the group's leader. In 1965 three Nation of Islam members shot him to death during a speech in New York City. After his death, more and more people learned about Malcolm X. His writings, particularly his book *The Autobiography of Malcolm X*, influenced Stokely Carmichael and other leaders of the Black Power movement.

■ UP IN FLAMES

In the northern and western United States, there were no segregation laws. But blacks in northern and western cities were segregated nevertheless. They usually lived in the inner city, where schools were run-down, crime and unemployment were high, and the police treated residents harshly. Whites lived in separate city neighborhoods or out in the suburbs.

The Watts neighborhood of Los Angeles was a typical big-city ghetto, largely home to poor blacks. In the summer of 1965, a confrontation between white police officers and a black motorist in Watts quickly escalated into violence.Fed up with police brutality, Watts residents started rioting. They set fire to buildings, looted white-owned businesses, and attacked the police with rocks and gunfire. After six days, the police and National Guard eventually restored order, but not before thirty-four people had died. Two summers later, more race riots broke out in more than one hundred other U.S. cities. The worst rioting occurred in Detroit, Michigan, where forty-three people died in seven days of violence.

DEMONSTRATORS CROWD AROUND A POLICE CAR in the Watts area of Los Angeles on August 12, 1965.

PRESIDENT LYNDON JOHNSON speaks to members of the Kerner Commission in late July 1967. Behind him stand Otto Kerner *(left)* and John Lindsay, the chairman and vice chairman, respectively, of the commission.

After the riots, President Johnson appointed a special commission to study the racial climate in big U.S. cities. Called the Kerner Commission, the group concluded that the United States was "moving toward two societies, one black and one white—separate and unequal."

Shortly after the Kerner Commission released its report, more tragedy occurred. In late March 1968, Martin Luther King Jr. was in Memphis, Tennessee, to support black sanitation workers. They had gone on strike as a tactic to win higher wages and better working conditions. In Memphis, King met with the workers, led a march to city hall, and gave a speech at the Mason Temple.

Throughout his career, King had received many death threats. White supremacists had once bombed his home. King got more threats in Memphis. Taking the threats very seriously, on April 3, King told the crowd at the Mason Temple that he might not live to see the results of his work. He also said that he wasn't afraid of being killed. He was happy just knowing that the civil rights struggle would succeed.

The next day, April 4, King stood with his colleagues on a balcony at the Lorraine Motel. Shots rang out, and King fell backward. Within an hour, he was pronounced dead at a nearby hospital. The killer, James Earl Ray, was captured several months later.

Shots rang out, and King fell backward. Within an hour, he was pronounced dead at a nearby hospital.

When news of King's death reached the public, people rioted in many cities. Others were simply stunned and sad. President Johnson declared April 7 to be a national day of mourning.

Martin Luther King Jr.'s assassination added to the deep wound in the American psyche. People were traumatized by war overseas and violence at home. Yet King's tragic death and his legacy inspired others. Using tactics learned from civil rights marchers, Hispanic Americans, American Indians, and other minorities began to organize and fight for their rights. The National Council of La Raza (the People), an organization of Hispanic Americans, formed in 1968. The American Indian Movement (AIM) also formed in 1968. Women, gays, and other oppressed minorities also began to organize in the late 1960s. By the 1970s, the days of the white, male stranglehold on U.S. power were over. A new era was well under way.

MARTIN LUTHER KING JR. LIES ON A BALCONY OF THE LORRAINE MOTEL in Memphis, Tennessee, after being shot. Standing over him are civil rights leaders Ralph Abernathy *(second from left)*, Andrew Young *(third from left)*, and Jesse Jackson *(fourth from left)*.

Cesar Chavez and Dolores Huerta paid close attention to the civil rights protests of the early 1960s. By watching African Americans in the South, they learned how nonviolent action could bring an end to injustice and help poor people improve their lives. Chavez and Huerta were community organizers in California. They worked with poor farmworkers, most of them Mexican American. These workers labored under the hot sun, picking fruit and vegetables. Their wages were rock bottom. They and their families lived in temporary camps, without decent housing, water, or sanitation. They moved from one farm to the next—wherever they could find work. The labor itself was grueling. Making matters worse, growers often sprayed their fields with dangerous pesticides that made workers sick. Chavez and Huerta were committed to improving life for farmworkers. They formed the National Farm Workers Association (NFWA) in 1962. Through this organization, workers began to organize and fight for better working conditions.

At first the group grew slowly. Then, on September 8, 1965, a group of Filipino farmworkers went on strike in Delano, California. The strike was designed to pressure grape growers to pay higher wages. Soon after, NFWA members joined the strike. They, too, refused to work for the grape growers. Strikers also staged nonviolent protests. Cesar Chavez even went on a hunger strike to call attention to the cause. To add more pressure, the strikers asked consumers to boycott, or refuse to buy, grapes. Many consumers responded, sales of grapes fell dramatically, and by 1969, growers were feeling the pinch. They agreed to negotiate with the farmworkers. The two sides signed a three-year contract. It included higher wages, medical clinics, and improved sanitation for workers. Growers also agreed to use less dangerous pesticides. The success of the grape boycott brought national acclaim to Chavez and Huerta. In the following decades, they continued to organize farmworkers. Cesar Chavez died in 1993. Dolores Huerta still works on behalf of poor Americans.

43

DOLORES HUERTA AND CESAR CHAVEZ were instrumental in gaining better working conditions for U.S. farmworkers.

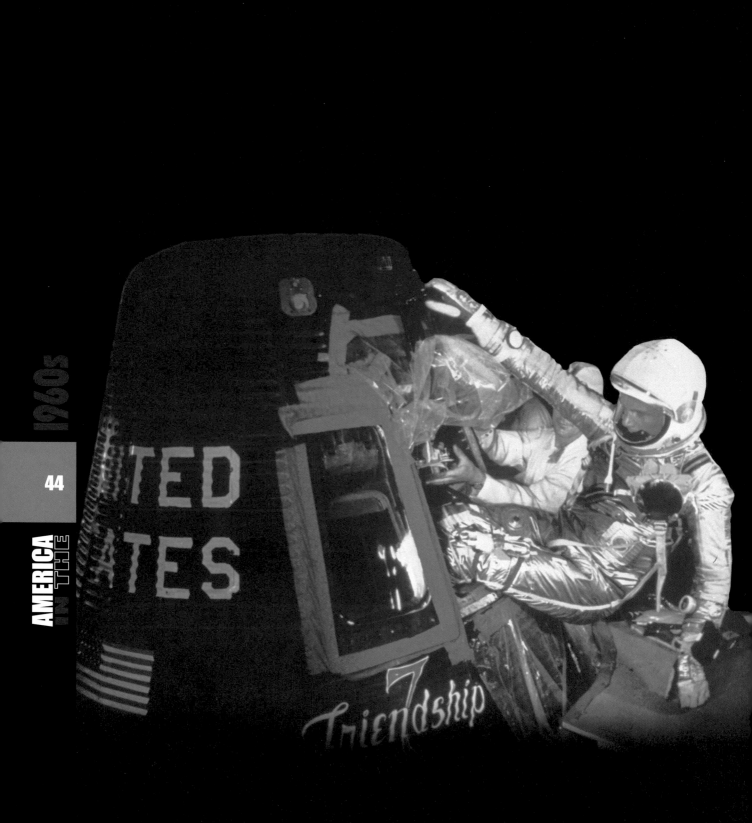

ASTRONAUT JOHN GLENN JR. enters *Friendship 7* in 1962 to prepare for launch.
He was the first American to orbit Earth.

CHAPTER THREE

"ONE GIANT LEAP FOR MANKIND":
SCIENCE AND TECHNOLOGY IN THE 1960s

In the spring of 1961, John F. Kennedy was stewing mad. The Soviet Union had scored another major victory in the space race. It had sent a man into orbit—something the United States had yet to do. Not only did the Soviet achievement make the United States look inferior, it also raised the threat of a cold war in space. Could the Soviets use their advanced space technology to attack the United States from outer space?

President Kennedy was determined to make up ground in the space race. On May 25, 1961, Kennedy told Congress, "I believe that this nation should commit itself to achieving the goal, before this decade is out, of landing a man on the moon and returning him safely to the earth." This bold challenge greatly excited Americans. In the next few years, Congress poured billions of dollars into the space program to make sure the goal would be met.

■ MOONSTRUCK

By 1961 the United States had already made great strides in space exploration. In the late 1950s, it had launched a series of satellites into orbit. The satellites carried cameras, radios, and other equipment that allowed scientists to study the world beyond Earth. Satellites had many uses. The U.S. military used satellites to spy on the Soviet Union from space. Weather forecasters used satellites to study Earth's upper atmosphere. Broadcasters used satellites to relay television signals across oceans.

"I believe that this nation should commit itself to achieving the goal, before this decade is out, of landing a man on the moon and returning him safely to the earth."

—President John F. Kennedy, May 1961

But the most exciting part of space exploration was the push to put a human on the moon. Throughout the 1960s, the United States made steady progress toward that goal. In February 1962, astronaut John Glenn became the first American to orbit Earth. In June 1965, Edward White became the first American to leave a spacecraft and "walk" in outer space. Meanwhile, the United States launched a series of unpiloted space probes to study the moon and prepare for the day when astronauts would land there.

That day was July 20, 1969, the craft was *Apollo 11*, and the first astronaut to set foot on the moon was Neil Armstrong. "That's one small step for [a] man, one giant leap for mankind," Armstrong said as he descended from the lunar module onto the moon's rocky surface. Television cameras sent the scene back to Earth. At home, Americans watched in wonder as the space-suited Armstrong and fellow astronaut Buzz Aldrin picked up moon rocks, took photographs, and planted a U.S. flag on the moon.

U.S. ASTRONAUT BUZZ ALDRIN ON THE SURFACE OF THE MOON, JULY 1969. Fellow moonwalker Neil Armstrong took this photograph.

n December 1968, U.S. astronauts William Anders, James Lovell, and Frank Borman were traveling aboard the *Apollo 8* spacecraft, in orbit around the moon. *Apollo 8* was one of several U.S. spaceflights that explored the moon in preparation for the *Apollo 11* landing in July 1969. As *Apollo 8* orbited the moon, Anders and Borman took pictures of the lunar surface. Scientists back on Earth were particularly interested in studying the far side of the moon, which human eyes had never seen before (although unpiloted spacecraft had photographed the far side). On December 24, 1968, as *Apollo 8* completed its fourth orbit around the moon, Frank Borman looked over the lunar horizon and shouted, "Oh my God, look at that picture over there! Here's the Earth coming up!" Quickly, he and Anders snapped pictures of Earth rising behind the moon. Borman took a black-and-white photo, and Anders took two color shots. The color images show Earth as a small blue globe, rising above the moon in a vast expanse of black space. Back on Earth, the earthrise shots made a sensation.

47

EARTH RISES OVER THE LUNAR HORIZON This image was captured in December 1968.

This time, it was the Soviet Union's turn to stew. In fact, Soviet leaders refused to broadcast the moon landing footage on Soviet television.

■ FIRSTS AND MORE FIRSTS

In the 1960s, the pace of U.S. life quickened. Cars and airplanes got bigger and faster. On television, Americans watched pivotal events— John F. Kennedy's funeral, combat in Vietnam, and the moon landing— shortly after they happened, sometimes even as they happened.

Meanwhile, industry cranked out new machines and new materials. An engineer named Theodore Maiman constructed the first laser in 1960. Lasers produce powerful beams of light—strong enough to cut metal. Engineers quickly used Maiman's invention in industry, medicine, and communications. In 1965 the DuPont Company created Kevlar—a stronger-than-steel fiber. It was used to strengthen tires, airplanes, boats, and bulletproof vests.

Computers were not new in the 1960s—government, universities, and businesses had been using them for years. But the early models were massive (some took up entire rooms), slow, and expensive. During the 1960s, engineers worked to make computers smaller, cheaper, and more powerful. The PDP-8, built by the Digital Equipment Corporation in 1965, was the first minicomputer. By modern standards, it was still gigantic—roughly the size of a small refrigerator—and very expensive at eighteen thousand dollars. But it represented a major step on the road to the small personal computers of later decades. The U.S. Defense Department developed the ARPAnet—the precursor to the modern Internet—in 1969.

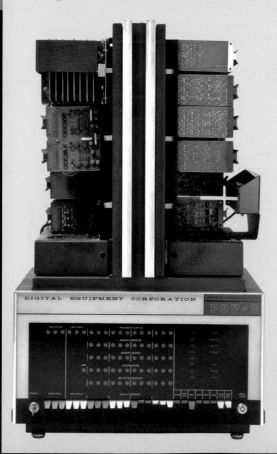

THE PDP-8, built in 1965, was the first minicomputer. It was the size of a small refrigerator.

Like computers, copy machines of the 1960s were big and expensive. The first mass-produced Xerox copier weighed 650 pounds (295 kilograms) and cost almost thirty thousand dollars. Still, copy machines and computers speeded up business operations. Consumers enjoyed many new products and services in the 1960s. In 1966 Procter & Gamble sold the first disposable diapers.

THE FIRST TOUCH-TONE TELEPHONE was introduced on February 28, 1963.

In 1963 AT&T introduced the first touch-tone telephones. These phones made calling quicker and easier—callers simply pushed buttons instead of turning old-fashioned rotary dials. The Early Bird, the world's first commercial communications satellite, went into orbit in 1965. This satellite made it easier to send telephone signals across oceans.

New medicines and medical technologies improved lives in the 1960s. The oral polio vaccine, developed by chemist Albert Sabin, was an advance on Jonas Salk's earlier injected vaccine. The oral vaccine gave people lifetime immunity against polio and eliminated the need for booster shots. Surgeons also made great strides in the 1960s. They used lasers to perform eye surgery and installed pacemakers in heart patients.

Perhaps the most influential medical advance of the 1960s was the birth control pill (commonly called the Pill). Searle, a pharmaceutical company, got government approval to sell the Pill in 1960. Within two years, more than one million U.S. women were taking the Pill every day. The Pill gave women more control over when and whether they became pregnant. It allowed them to make their own decisions about sex, reproduction, and family size. In that way, it set the stage for the feminist movement of the mid-1960s.

■ SCIENCE IN THE KITCHEN

Fast food was not a new idea in the 1960s. Americans had been eating at McDonald's and other chain restaurants since the 1950s. People had been enjoying TV dinners (just heat and serve) since the 1950s too.

But fast food got much faster in the 1960s. Americans bought more and more ready-made food. Carnation Instant Breakfast was new in the 1960s. So were instant mashed potatoes and Shake 'n Bake, a premade breading for chicken. To help people cook new foods faster, the Amana Company introduced the home microwave oven in 1967. New fast-food chains included Arby's (founded in 1964) and Wendy's (1969).

As the decade went on, a larger portion of the U.S. diet came from processed foods. But many of the new foods contained some not-so-wholesome ingredients. TaB, for instance, is a diet cola introduced by the Coca-Cola Company in 1963. Sugar-free, TaB got its sweetness from a chemical called cyclamate. In the late 1960s, researchers discovered that cyclamate could cause cancer. The government banned the use of cyclamate in foods. But TaB was wildly popular, so the company switched to a different kind of artificial sweetener, saccharine. Some studies suggested that saccharine could cause cancer too, but people kept drinking TaB and other sugar-free soft drinks.

Americans were space crazy in the 1960s, and lots of kids wanted to eat what the astronauts ate. The most popular "space food" was Tang, a sweet powdered drink. Astronauts drank Tang on the Gemini spaceflights, and the General Foods Corporation used Tang's space appeal to sell it hand over fist to U.S. kids. Space Food Sticks were chewy energy bars

A saleswoman demonstrates a **MICROWAVE OVEN** in the late 1960s. Microwaves were a revolutionary way to cook.

created by the Pillsbury Company. They fed moon-bound astronauts and Earthbound Americans alike.

Despite the rush to fast and processed foods, many Americans of the 1960s still cooked the old-fashioned way—with raw, unprocessed ingredients. In fact, one of the most popular television shows of the 1960s was *The French Chef*. The show starred chef Julia Child. She showed viewers how to make beef bourguignone, bouillabaisse à la Marseillaise, and other French dishes that lots of viewers couldn't pronounce—but wanted to learn how to make at home.

■ THE DARK SIDE

Much technology of the 1960s was beneficial to humans. Some of it was out-and-out harmful, however. Nuclear technology was particularly sinister—although many Americans didn't know it at the time. After World War II, the U.S. government tested nuclear bombs in remote places in Nevada and Alaska. The bombs released radioactive fallout, or particles, into the air, water, and soil near test sites. The particles sickened plants, people, and animals. Many people died of cancer caused by nuclear fallout. And because radioactive particles remain

in the environment for many years (thousands and even billions of years in some cases), people continued to get sick, long after the tests were done. Nuclear technology was new, and at first, even scientists didn't realize how dangerous it was.

Gradually, people learned about the dangers. The National Committee for SANE Nuclear Policy, formed in 1957, took the lead in protesting against nuclear bombs and nuclear testing. The antinuclear forces achieved a big victory in 1963 when the United States, the Soviet Union, and the United Kingdom signed the Limited Test Ban Treaty. This treaty banned the testing of nuclear weapons in the atmosphere, in outer space, and underwater. Only underground tests were still allowed.

Around this time, Americans learned about other environmental contaminants. One example was acid rain, or rainwater containing air pollution. When acid rain falls from the sky, it contaminates lakes, streams, and forests where it falls. It can harm and even kill the plants and animals that live in these places. In 1962 a U.S. folksinger named Malvina Reynolds wrote a song called "What Have They Done to the Rain?"

AMERICA IN THE 1960s

Ralph Nader learned about politics early on. At his boyhood home in Connecticut, his parents—both immigrants from Lebanon—often lectured their children about the responsibilities of citizens in a democracy. After high school, Nader studied government and economics at Princeton University in New Jersey. Then he enrolled in Harvard Law School in Massachusetts.

As a young lawyer in Connecticut, Nader realized that big U.S. corporations often act selfishly—purely to make money and not in the best interests of the consumers who buy their products. Nader began to investigate the U.S. auto industry. He discovered that some U.S. cars were unsafe and that auto executives resisted spending money on safety features. In 1965 Nader published his findings in a book called *Unsafe at Any Speed: The Designed-In Dangers of the American Automobile*. The book catapulted Nader to fame but also aroused the wrath of the auto industry. General Motors even hired private detectives to tap Nader's telephone and dig up dirt on his personal life.

In 1968 Nader founded the Center for Study of Responsive Law (CSRL) in Washington, D.C. Hundreds of young lawyers and researchers flocked to Washington to join the organization. Nicknamed Nader's Raiders, CSRL staffers investigated air and water pollution, unsafe products, and

RALPH NADER worked throughout the 1960s and much of his life as a consumer protection advocate.

government corruption. Their work helped lead to the creation of the Environmental Protection Agency, the Occupational Safety and Health Administration, the Consumer Product Safety Commission, and other government agencies. Nader worked as a consumer advocate throughout the rest of the twentieth century and into the twenty-first. He wrote books and articles, founded consumer organizations, and fought on behalf of consumers, minorities, the environment, and the poor. Nader ran for president in 1996, 2000, 2004, and 2008.

In it, Reynolds laments that something as precious and pure as rainwater could become dangerous and destructive.

Rachel Carson was another American who sounded the alarm about pollution. She focused on DDT, a chemical used to kill insects on crops. But DDT can also kill plants, birds, fish, and other animals. DDT can harm people when they eat contaminated plants and animals. In 1962 Carson wrote a book called *Silent Spring*. This book called attention to the dangers of pesticide use and demanded change. Carson was a pioneer in the growing U.S. environmental movement. Slowly, people were learning that Earth and its creatures needed protection.

Many young people were active in the environmental protection movement. Some ate only natural, unprocessed foods. Others ate no meat. Some moved to the countryside, where they grew their own food and shunned most modern technology. A popular book called the *Whole Earth Catalog* taught people how to live off the land, make their own tools, and live in harmony with nature.

Back in the cities, people pressured the U.S. government to pass environmental protection laws. In 1970 the government established the Environmental Protection Agency. The office is in charge of preventing, cleaning up, and setting limits on air, water, and other kinds of pollution.

RACHEL CARSON TELLS lawmakers about the danger of pesticides in 1963.

ROBERT KENNEDY *(right)* visits a playground in the Bedford-Stuyvesant neighborhood of Brooklyn, New York, in 1966 to gain a better understanding of the struggles poor Americans faced.

CHAPTER FOUR

THE GREAT SOCIETY:
THE 1960s ECONOMY

For most Americans, the 1960s was a prosperous decade. The economy had boomed after World War II and continued to boom in the decades that followed. In the early 1960s, the gross national product—the measure of all goods and services produced in the nation in one year—grew by 5 percent each year. Incomes rose and unemployment fell.

With their big cars, suburban homes, credit cards, and backyard barbecues, many Americans were well contented. The government also had money to spend—on space exploration, national defense, and the Vietnam War, for example. Companies such as Ford, IBM, and General Foods saw profits pile up as Americans enjoyed new technology and seemingly endless choices at the corner store.

But not everyone was wealthy or even comfortable in the 1960s. Black Americans had benefited little from postwar prosperity. Some white Americans also struggled. When Robert Kennedy visited towns in the Appalachian Mountains or the inner cities of big urban areas, he encountered children "whose bellies are swollen with hunger . . . who have never been to school, never seen a doctor or a dentist . . . never read or even seen a book." One study showed that in big cities such as Chicago and New York, black unemployment was double that of white unemployment. Another study revealed that more than 40 percent of nonwhite Americans were living below the poverty line.

55

■ THE WAR ON POVERTY

President Johnson believed that the United States had an obligation to help poor people. He spoke of a Great Society—a society in which everyone enjoyed a good education, racial justice, and the fruits of U.S. prosperity.

"The Great Society rests on abundance and liberty for all," Johnson told University of Michigan graduates in 1964. "It demands an end to poverty and racial injustice. . . . The Great Society is a place where every child can find knowledge to enrich his mind and to enlarge his talents. . . . It is a place where man can renew contact with nature. . . . It is a place where men are more concerned with the quality of their goals than the quantity of their goods."

To create the Great Society, Johnson declared a "War on Poverty." He spearheaded a number of laws and social programs to help the needy. These well-known and far-reaching programs included Medicare (health care for senior citizens), Medicaid (health care for the poor), Head Start (preschool and social services to poor children), and employment programs such as the Job Corps. The Civil Rights Act of 1964 and the Voting Rights Act of 1965 were also part of Johnson's Great Society vision.

The Great Society programs were possible, in part, because of the booming U.S. economy of the 1960s. The nation was rich, and the government had plenty of money to spend on social programs. The Great Society appeared to be a success, at least at first. In 1960, 22 percent of Americans were living below the poverty line. By 1969 that number had fallen to 12 percent.

A TEACHER LEADS A HEAD START PROGRAM in the mid-1960s. The program aimed to help poor children catch up academically with their wealthier classmates.

HOW FAR WOULD A DOLLAR GO in the 1960s?

	1960s	2000s (first decade)
Average U.S. worker's income	$6,162	$40,000

TYPICAL PRICES

	1960s	2000s
Pack of chewing gum	5¢	79¢
Loaf of bread	19¢	$2.79
Quart of milk	29¢	$1.79
Jar of peanut butter	51¢	$2.69
Six pack of Pepsi	59¢	$2.99
Movie ticket	75¢	$9.00
Man's haircut	$2.50	$30.00
Pair of men's shoes	$16.95	$79.99
Child's bicycle	$37.85	$139.99
Washing machine	$249.95	$809.99
Color television set	$629.95	$329.99
Two-door car	$3,100	$20,000
Three-bedroom house	$23,500	$300,000

(Prices are samples only. At any given time, prices vary by year, location, size, brand, and model.)

■ BREAKING THE BANK

By the late 1960s, it had become clear that post–World War II prosperity wouldn't go on forever. As the war in Vietnam dragged on and on, it began to take a toll on the nation's budget. To pay for the war, the government had to raise taxes. The economy slowed. The national debt grew. Prices started to rise—a trend called inflation.

As the 1960s rolled over into the 1970s, the United States found itself in an economic recession, or slowdown. Good times certainly hadn't ended—but they weren't quite so good as before.

THE ROLE OF AMERICAN WOMEN as full-time homemakers underwent great changes in the 1960s.

CHAPTER FIVE

LIBERATION!
SOCIAL CHANGE IN THE 1960s

In 1956 *Life* magazine devoted an entire issue to U.S. women. What was their proper role in society and the family? Should women have careers? According to four male doctors interviewed by the magazine, "The children are *her* [the mother's] responsibility. Daddy is busy, he understands business, she understands children." Women, the doctors continued, had "a primitive biological urge toward reproduction, toward homemaking and nurturing." The doctors concluded that women with careers were a menace to the U.S. family—their children would become juvenile delinquents, atheists, Communists, and homosexuals.

Betty Friedan could not have disagreed more. A journalist and mother of three, she thought the magazine had it all wrong. There was more to a woman's life than marriage and motherhood, she said. To be fulfilled, women also needed education and careers. Friedan elaborated on these ideas in a 1963 book, *The Feminine Mystique*.

Friedan's book began by describing the frustration of a typical suburban housewife: "As she made the beds, shopped for groceries, matched slipcover material, ate peanut butter sandwiches with her children, chauffeured Cub Scouts and Brownies, lay beside her husband at night—she was afraid to ask even of herself the silent question—'Is this all?'" For U.S. women at the tail end of the baby boom, *The Feminine Mystique* hit a nerve. They agreed with Friedan: There had to be more to life than scrubbing floors, washing clothes, and cooking meals.

Inspired by Friedan's work, women began to examine inequities between the sexes. For the most part, U.S. men worked at paying jobs and made business decisions, while women cared for the home and children. And for women who did work outside the home, the inequities were great: Men earned more money than women—even for the same jobs. Some employers fired women when they got married or got pregnant. Others fired women who lost their sex appeal. For instance, flight attendants (who were all female and were called stewardesses in those days) could be fired if they gained too much weight or got too old.

Job listings in newspapers were segregated by sex. Under "Help Wanted—Female," the job offerings were generally low paying: waitress, shop clerk, and secretary. "Help Wanted—Male" listed higher-paying, professional jobs—manager, engineer, and real estate agent—as well as jobs considered inappropriate for women, such as truck driver. A woman who wanted to attend law school, medical school, or another professional training program in the 1960s often found herself barred from enrollment simply because of her sex. And even within the civil rights and antiwar movements—the centers of the fight for justice and equality—women were usually restricted to secretarial work, while men held leadership positions.

BETTY FRIEDAN speaks to a group of people about sexual discrimination in 1966.

I n the 1960s, nothing represented traditional womanhood in the United States more than the Miss America Pageant. The pageant was wholesome family entertainment. The pretty, upbeat contestants—all of them white—showed off for the judges. They paraded in swimsuits and evening gowns. They displayed talents such as baton twirling, singing, and piano playing. The young contestants were not hippies or radical feminists. They did not want to change the world—they simply wanted to put on a good show. And part of that show included parading their legs and curvy figures before a TV audience. But for Robin Morgan, a leading feminist of the 1960s, the Miss America Pageant was nothing more than exploitation. The pageant treated women purely as sex objects, Morgan said, judged exclusively on their good looks.

At the 1968 Miss America Pageant in Atlantic City, New Jersey, Morgan and about one hundred fellow feminists staged a dramatic protest. Outside the pageant hall, they sang songs, waved posters, and shouted "Liberation Now!" They even held an alternative pageant, at which they

PICKETERS PROTEST THE ANNUAL MISS AMERICA PAGEANT in Atlantic City, New Jersey, in 1968.

crowned a sheep as their "Miss America," explaining that the human contestants were "oppressed and judged like animals at the county fair." The protesters also filled a trash can with items that represented the exploitation of women. These items included spike-heeled shoes, girdles, hair curlers, false eyelashes, women's magazines such as *Ladies' Home Journal*, and men's magazines like *Playboy*. But soon an angry, mostly male crowd gathered. The men drowned out the protesters with their own jeers and sexist insults. The protest made headlines, but it was clear from the backlash that day that women still had a long way to go in their fight for respect and equality.

■ WHEN DO WE WANT IT? NOW!

Awakened to this injustice, Friedan and other activists began to lobby Congress for equal rights for women. Their efforts led to the passage of two new laws—the Equal Pay Act of 1963 and Title VII of the Civil Rights Act of 1964. These laws were designed to eliminate sex discrimination in pay and hiring. But attitudes were slow to change. Many employers failed to follow the laws, and government enforcement was lax.

So Betty Friedan and her colleagues in the women's rights movement decided to take bolder action. They created the National Organization for Women (NOW) in 1966. The following year, NOW drafted a "Bill of Rights for Women." The bill included eight demands: passage of an Equal Rights (for women) Amendment to the U.S. Constitution, stricter enforcement of laws against sex discrimination in the workplace, guaranteed maternity leave for working mothers, tax deductions for home and child care expenses for working parents, government-funded day care centers, equal treatment of women in education, job training for poor women, and the right of women to access birth control and have abortions.

Ten years earlier, these demands would have been unthinkable. But U.S. society was changing. By then blacks were demanding equal rights. Hispanics and Native Americans were demanding equal rights. And women were doing the same. Old ideas about sex, gender, and family were falling by the wayside. For young women, marriage and motherhood were no longer the only choices. Women began to pursue professional careers. Some postponed marriage and childbirth. Others chose not to marry at all. In earlier decades, people were ashamed if their marriages ended in divorce. But divorce rates rose in the 1960s, as both men and women realized there was no benefit in staying in an unhappy marriage and no shame in leaving one.

> U.S. society was changing.... Old ideas about sex, gender, and family were falling by the wayside. For young women, marriage and motherhood were no longer the only choices.

■ DO YOUR OWN THING

Perhaps it started with rock-and-roll music. Or with the beatniks of New York and San Francisco. However it started, a new movement was afoot by the mid-1960s. Young people were starting to rebel. They were protesting the Vietnam War and resisting the draft. They were joining the civil rights struggle. Most of all, they were rejecting the values of their parents and their government. To many, living the "straight" life—military service, a college education, a steady job with a big company, and a traditional marriage with kids—didn't look appealing. Young people wanted something different—and they began to express that difference in many ways.

First, young people wanted to *look* different. Young men grew long hair and beards. They cast aside neat slacks, sport jackets, suits, and ties in favor of bell-bottom blue jeans, T-shirts, and sandals. Young women replaced their trim, tailored skirts and blouses with jeans and colorful free-flowing dresses. They ditched prim hairdos and let their hair flow long.

Accessories such as flowers, headbands, "love beads," and "granny glasses" completed the new look.

Besides long hair and colorful clothing, young people also listened to rock-and-roll music in the 1960s. Many experimented with drugs, especially marijuana. Some decided to "drop out" of society. They hitchhiked around Europe or drove across the United States in Volkswagen vans. Others moved to rural areas and set up communes, or group households. On college campuses, students printed "underground newspapers,"

63

TWO HIPPIES stand in San Francisco's Golden Gate Park during one of the many festivals held there during the summer of 1967.

filled with radical, alternative political messages. Everywhere, young people searched out new ideas and new ways of looking at life.

In earlier generations, many young women had resisted having sex before marriage. To do so would have ruined their reputations as "nice girls" and risked a shameful pregnancy. For youth of the 1960s, such restrictions were a thing of the past. Many young women took birth control pills to prevent pregnancy. They freely explored their sexual feelings. Sex before marriage was no longer taboo. Young people extolled the benefits of "free love"—that is, making love without marriage or long-term commitments.

Not all young people wore long hair, listened to rock and roll, and took drugs in the 1960s. Many were quite conservative. They dutifully volunteered for service in Vietnam. They dressed and behaved just as their parents' generation had. But these youths didn't make headlines. It was those who rebelled who got all the media attention. The press called them hippies—a name that many young people wore proudly. Later, people would use the term *counterculture* to describe the 1960s youth movement.

Hippies and peace protesters were often one and the same. At antiwar demonstrations, hippies often staged attention-grabbing stunts, such as blowing soap bubbles at police, inserting flowers into the barrels of soldiers' guns and, on one occasion, attempting to levitate (lift up) the Pentagon with the sheer power of thought. The term *flower power* was popular with hippies. It was the power to bring about change through love and peace.

Although hippies were actually a small fraction of American youth in the 1960s, they made a big cultural impact—on fashion, music, art, and politics. And when hippies got together—for instance, during the "Human Be-in" or the "Summer of Love" in San Francisco in 1967 or at the Woodstock music festival in upstate New York in 1969—it seemed as if they had taken over the nation.

■ GENERATION GAP

"You can't trust anybody over thirty," hippie activists said in the 1960s. At the same time, older people were wary of anyone *under* thirty. To many older Americans, it seemed as if the youth of the 1960s had lost their minds. Young people appeared to be throwing everything sacred—

"You can't trust anyone over thirty."

—Hippie motto, 1960s

marriage, patriotism, and respect for authority—out the window. They insulted the government, the president, and the police. They took drugs, dressed in tattered clothing, used foul language, and talked openly about sex. For many Americans, this behavior was unacceptable.

So it came as no surprise when more conservative Americans fought back. Hippies and protesters were nothing more than "spoiled, deluded, arrogant, brainwashed brats and know-it-alls," wrote one conservative columnist. Others called them Communists and traitors to the United States. Some restaurants refused to serve anyone with long hair, beards, or sandals. The police frequently raided underground newspapers and harassed hippie hitchhikers. Many Americans thought hippies were simply dirty and lazy. "You shout four letter words at me," said segregationist George Wallace to young protesters during his campaign for president. "Well I have two for you." Then he spelled them out: *S-O-A-P* and *W-O-R-K*.

PROTESTERS FACE MILITARY POLICE during an antiwar demonstration near the Pentagon in 1967.

mericans of earlier decades had many taboos—and one of the biggest was homosexuality. Gay people kept their sexuality a secret. If they came out openly as gay, they were likely to lose their jobs or face violence. People who entered into same-sex relationships could be arrested for "deviant behavior." Going to a gay bar was risky. Police often raided gay bars and threw bar customers in jail. On the night of June 27, 1969, the police made one of their regular raids on the Stonewall Inn, a bar for gay men in New York City. The officers began making arrests, expecting no resistance from the customers, as was usually the case. But as the officers led the arrested men to a waiting police wagon, gay men from the surrounding neighborhood began to gather outside the bar. The crowd grew angry. Some of the arrested men tried to escape, and the crowd then turned on the officers, pelting them with bricks and trash. The police called in an antiriot squad, which eventually restored calm.

The next night, a larger crowd gathered outside the Stonewall. This time, a chant arose from the crowd: "Gay Power, Gay Power." When the police arrived, the crowd threw rocks and bottles. After a few days, peace returned to the neighborhood. But

GAY PATRONS RESIST A POLICE RAID at the Stonewall Inn on June 27, 1969. The event became known as the Stonewall Riots.

the larger gay community would never be the same. After the riots, a great weight of shame and secrecy began to lift off the shoulders of gay Americans. They would no longer fearfully submit to discrimination. Instead, they began to proudly proclaim their sexuality. They formed groups such as the Gay Liberation Front, a pioneer in the fight for gay rights. The early gay rights movement fit well with other social changes of the 1960s, since people were reevaluating gender, sexuality, and romantic relationships on all levels. The struggle for gay equality continues. Every June, gay people gather in cities throughout the United States to remember the Stonewall Riots and the birth of the gay rights movement.

■ ONE NATION UNDER GOD?

For almost two hundred years, Protestantism dominated in the United States. Church and state were separated, but non-Protestants sometimes suffered discrimination in business, housing, and education. But along with everything else in the 1960s in the United States, religious views changed. Americans became more tolerant of people of minority religions—be it Judaism, Catholicism, or other religions. Some Americans wouldn't vote for John F. Kennedy because he was Catholic. But Kennedy still won the 1960 election, breaking a barrier as the nation's first (and, so far, only) Catholic president. Jews entered business, politics, and other professional jobs in greater numbers than ever before in the 1960s.

Religion and politics are often intertwined—and that was certainly true in the 1960s. Church leaders such as Martin Luther King Jr. were also leaders in the civil rights struggle. Many pacifists and war protesters, such as Daniel and Philip Berrigan, were religious leaders as well. Their antiwar philosophies had a basis in religious teaching.

Along with the rest of society, churches grew more tolerant of new ideas, new roles for women, and new political views in the 1960s. Even the rule-bound Catholic Church made changes. In the early 1960s, Catholic leaders in Rome, Italy, held a series of meetings called Vatican II. The leaders enacted various changes in church policy, including saying Mass in English and other local languages instead of Latin.

Some Americans, especially members of the counterculture, broke with the religions of their birth in the 1960s. Many young people who had been raised as Christians or Jews left those faiths. They explored Eastern religions such as Taoism, Hinduism, and Zen Buddhism.

Beginning in 1960, Madalyn Murray O'Hair led a Supreme Court fight against prayer in the public schools, based on the Constitutional principle of separation of church and state. In 1963 she founded a group called American Atheists Inc. (Atheists believe there is no god.) Americans had become tolerant of religious difference, but many people drew the line at rejecting religion altogether. O'Hair received angry threats and hate mail. *Life* magazine christened her "the most hated woman in America."

Poet and activist ALLEN GINSBURG speaks in Washington Square Park in New York City.

CHAPTER SIX

VOICES:
WRITING OF THE 1960s

In the 1960s, U.S. literature and journalism, like everything else in society, changed radically. Some writers blurred the difference between fact and fiction. Others introduced new kinds of storytelling. Women and minorities added their voices to U.S. literature in ways that had never been done before.

The Beats were one of the most influential literary movements of the 1960s. This loosely knit group of writers had started working in the 1950s. Their literary styles and lifestyles helped set the stage for the 1960s counterculture. The Beats were inspired by jazz music, Eastern philosophy and religion, drug use, and the Bohemian life. The two most important Beat writers were the novelist Jack Kerouac and the poet Allen Ginsberg.

Kerouac's novel *On the Road* was a huge best seller when it came out in 1957. The book offered an autobiographical account of a cross-country car trip. Young readers responded passionately to the novel's unconventional writing style and antiauthoritarian message. In the 1960s, Kerouac published numerous other works—both prose and poetry. They included *Tristessa, Book of Dreams, Big Sur, Visions of Cody, Visions of Gerard,* and V*anity of Duluoz.* None achieved the critical acclaim or popularity of *On the Road.* But it didn't matter. By the 1960s,

Beat writer **JACK KEROUAC** influenced many young people in the 1960s.

Jack Kerouac was already a hero to the growing youth movement. Inspired by Kerouac, thousands of young people embarked on their own cross-country road trips.

The charismatic poet Allen Ginsberg was another Beat legend. Beat poetry had developed in big-city coffeehouses, where poets read their works aloud. The Beat style featured repetition, unusual rhythms and patterns—often borrowed from jazz music—and sometimes angry, shocking words. In 1956 Ginsberg had caused a sensation with his experimental poem "Howl," which contains many frank references to sex and drug use. He continued to write and recite poetry in the 1960s. He wrote *Kaddish* in 1961 and published a poetry collection called *Reality Sandwiches* in 1963. Ginsberg also embraced the hippie scene and the antiwar movement. He often played a key role at Vietnam War protests.

■ POLITICS ON PAPER

In 1960 journalist Theodore H. White had an interesting idea for a book. He wanted to document the presidential campaigns of Richard Nixon and John F. Kennedy. Both campaigns gave White intimate access to the candidates and their staffs. White then recorded behind-the-scenes campaign action and the dramatic 1960 election, one of the closest in U.S. history. The resulting book, *The Making of the President, 1960*, combined personal storytelling with ordinary reporting. The narrative involved the reader emotionally, offering insight into history as it unfolded. White's book became an instant best seller and a classic. He followed up this book with two more *Making of the President* titles, in 1968 and 1972.

By 1964 the most important job in U.S. journalism was reporting on the growing conflict in Vietnam. Many outstanding U.S. journalists made their names with dispatches from that war. In the early 1960s, David Halberstam covered the Vietnam War for the *New York Times*. This work earned him a Pulitzer Prize in journalism in 1964. Later, Halberstam published *The Best and the Brightest*, which chronicled how U.S. leaders had pushed the nation deep into the war in Vietnam.

In November 1969, journalist Seymour Hersh broke a shocking story in the U.S. press. Hersh reported that the previous year, U.S. soldiers had massacred more than four hundred Vietnamese civilians—unarmed women, children, and old men—in the village of My Lai in South Vietnam. What's more, the U.S. military had deliberately tried to keep the incident a secret. When Hersh's story hit newsstands, it sent a shock wave through U.S. society. It added explosive fuel to the antiwar movement, which by then had reached a fever pitch.

JOURNALIST DAVID HALBERSTAM slogged through the jungles of Vietnam to cover the war.

Marshall McLuhan came to fame in the 1960s by examining the modern media. McLuhan was born and worked mostly in Canada, but he had widespread influence in the United States. He began his career as an English professor. Early in his teaching career, McLuhan became interested in media and how it affects society. He focused his studies on electronic communication—particularly television. McLuhan noted that by the late twentieth century, the electronic age had replaced the age of print. He said that television and other high-speed media connected people around the world, creating a "global village." McLuhan wrote about his ideas in several popular books, including *Understanding Media* (1964), *The Medium Is the Massage* (1967), and *War and Peace in the Global Village* (1968). (Interestingly, *The Medium Is the Massage* was supposed to be *The Medium Is the Message*. The printer made a typo, and McLuhan liked it and left it.) With his sharp, cynical analy-

MARSHALL MCLUHAN wrote about the media in the 1960s.

sis of modern society, McLuhan became a counterculture favorite. His books were big sellers, and people flocked to hear him speak. He spent most of his career as a professor at the University of Toronto. He died in 1980.

■ NEW JOURNALISM

In the early 1960s, a group of writers, mostly in New York City and writing for magazines such as the *New Yorker* and *Esquire*, pushed nonfiction writing in a new direction. Their style was called New Journalism. New Journalism was nonfiction writing that incorporated literary techniques—extensive dialogue, first-person narrative, and vivid scene setting. Stories written this way were factual, but they were more dramatic and immediate than

"There goes (VAROOM! VAROOM!) that Kandy Kolored (THPHHHHHH!) tangerine-flake streamline baby (RAHGHHHH!) around the bend (BRUMMMMMMMMMMMMMMMMMM)"

—Tom Wolfe article headline (an early example of New Journalism), **Esquire** *magazine, 1963*

traditional nonfiction. Many world-famous writers rose to fame using New Journalism techniques. They include Tom Wolfe, Hunter S. Thompson, Norman Mailer, Joan Didion, and George Plimpton.

Although much New Journalism appeared in magazines, it also appeared in book form. Truman Capote's *In Cold Blood* is an example. In this book from 1966, Capote (who came to fame as a novelist in the 1950s) uses techniques of fiction writing to describe a real-life multiple murder in Kansas.

Norman Mailer also used the New Journalism approach in the 1960s. *His Armies of the Night* (1968) describes Mailer's experiences during an antiwar march in 1967. *Miami and the Siege of Chicago*, also from 1968, recounts the 1968 Republican and Democratic presidential conventions.

Writer Tom Wolfe, another New Journalism pioneer, was famous for his biting wit. In *The Kandy-Kolored Tangerine-Flake Streamline Baby* (1965), a collection of essays, Wolfe mocked 1960s culture, including fashion, art, and rock and roll. In *The Electric Kool-Aid Acid Test* (1968),

TOM WOLFE, wearing his signature white suit and shoes, stands on a street corner in New York City in 1968.

Wolfe took a close-up look at the counterculture. The book tells the true story of novelist Ken Kesey and a group of hippies traveling cross-country in a brightly painted school bus.

■ THE FACT OF FICTION

The fiction of the 1960s reflected the era's turbulence, and many novelists used humor to shed light on political and social conflict. Ken Kesey's classic *One Flew over the Cuckoo's Nest* (1962) takes place in a mental hospital in which the caretakers seem more disturbed than the patients. Richard Brautigan's *Trout Fishing in America* (1967), another sixties classic, is a whimsical and fantastic story that has very little to do with trout fishing. Thomas Pynchon, John Barth, and Donald Barthelme also combined comedy and fantasy to create brilliant works of fiction in the 1960s.

Many writers of the 1960s came of age during World War II, and their experiences in that war emerged in their novels. Joseph Heller's *Catch-22*, which appeared in 1961, follows the exploits of a fictional bomber squadron in Italy

Novelist **KEN KESEY** *(center)* talks to a group of his fans.

during the war. Kurt Vonnegut's *Slaughterhouse-Five* (1969) describes the horrific World War II firebombing of Dresden, Germany. Vonnegut tells the story through the eyes of Billy Pilgrim, a U.S. soldier and a prisoner of war during the bombing, just as Vonnegut was in his own life. Both novels use dark humor to expose the absurdity of war.

◼ THE BEAT GOES ON

When the 1960s began, many poets used a traditional approach to poetry writing, with rhyming words and lines written in predictable patterns. But as the decade wore on, poets began to use more experimental styles. Some were influenced by Allen Ginsberg and other Beat poets. Others responded to new trends in music and film. Some poets embraced a movement called surrealism. They tried to express the world of emotions using vivid, dreamlike imagery.

One of the most acclaimed poets (and novelists) of the 1960s was Sylvia Plath. Born in 1932, Plath studied at Smith College in Massachusetts and at Cambridge University in Great Britain. In Great Britain, she met and married poet Ted Hughes, with whom she had two children. Plath's novel *The Bell Jar* (1963) reflected many of her own deep emotional problems. After she and Hughes separated, Plath fell into despair. She managed to produce a brilliant series of poems before committing suicide in 1963. The poems were collected in the volume *Ariel* (1965) two years after her death.

SYLVIA PLATH was a prolific poet and journal writer. Her journals were first published in 1982.

■ *NOBODY KNOWS MY NAME*

The 1960s was a time of growing black pride. African American writers expressed that pride—as well as their frustrations—in poems, plays, and novels. Poets such as Maya Angelou and Nikki Giovanni wrote about their struggles as black women in the United States. Amiri Baraka, originally named LeRoi Jones, was the best-known African American poet of the 1960s. His works reflect the struggle for black pride and black power. Baraka also wrote plays. Ishmael Reed began his writing career with the *East Village Other*, an underground newspaper. He went on to write plays, poetry, and novels. His work, too, examines the lives of black Americans and their struggles with oppression and injustice.

African American writers expressed that pride—as well as their frustrations— in poems, plays, and novels.

As a black homosexual, James Baldwin experienced discrimination on two levels. For a time, Baldwin lived in France, where he could live more freely as a black man and a gay man. Beginning in the 1950s, Baldwin wrote about the struggles of black Americans. His most famous works of the 1960s include the essay collections *Nobody Knows My Name* and *The Fire Next Time*, the play *Blues for Mister Charlie*, the novels *Another Country* and *Tell Me How Long the Train's Been Gone*, and a collection of short stories, *Going to Meet the Man*.

JAMES BALDWIN hit his literary stride in the 1960s.

The Black Power movement inspired many writers of the 1960s. Nikki Giovanni was one of them. She was born Yolanda Cornelia Giovanni in Knoxville, Tennessee. She grew up in Cincinnati, Ohio. She entered Fisk University, an all-black college in Tennessee, in 1960. She dropped out but returned to the school several years later. By then the civil rights movement was in high gear.

At Fisk, Giovanni was active in the Student Nonviolent Coordinating Committee. She also joined the Fisk Writers Workshop and edited the school's literary magazine.

NIKKI GIOVANNI joined the Black Power movement in the 1960s.

77

With the assassination of Malcolm X, Giovanni became more and more militant. She wrote about racial prejudice and social injustice. She spoke of a Black Revolution, in which African Americans would stand up against white oppression. Her first book of poetry, *Black Feeling, Black Talk*, came out in 1968. She followed that up with *Black Judgment* in 1969 and *Re:Creation* in 1970. Giovanni went on to have a successful writing and teaching career. Over time, her work shifted away from black radicalism to themes such as motherhood, family, love, and loneliness. In 1987 she joined the faculty at Virginia Tech University in Blacksburg, where she teaches English. In addition to poetry, she has written numerous essays and children's books. She has received countless awards and honors for her work.

■ WOMEN'S WORDS

A host of women writers achieved success in the 1960s. Harper Lee, a native of Alabama, published her only novel, *To Kill a Mockingbird*, in 1960. The book is a masterpiece about the South and its legacy of racial hatred. Another southern writer, Georgia's Flannery O'Connor, rose to fame in the 1950s. In

1960 she published *The Violent Bear It Away*, her second novel. *Everything That Rises Must Converge*, a collection of her short stories, came out in 1965, a year after her death. The wildly prolific Joyce Carol Oates published four novels, two short story collections, and one poetry collection in the 1960s. The following decades saw her churn out dozens of additional works.

Susan Sontag and Joan Didion achieved fame as essayists in the 1960s. Didion's work, including her famous *Slouching Towards Bethlehem* (1968), explored the 1960s counterculture. Sontag's writings, such as *Against Interpretation* (1966), were more academic.

Some women in the 1960s explored women's lives directly. Helen Gurley Brown raised many eyebrows with her *Sex and the Single Girl* in 1962. Certainly, women had sex before marriage in the early 1960s—but it was still controversial. Brown's book (an instant best seller) changed all that. Brown encouraged single women to celebrate and enjoy their sex lives. She became

JOAN DIDION explored the 1960s counterculture firsthand by attending a hippie gathering at Golden Gate Park in San Francisco in 1967.

editor in chief of *Cosmopolitan* magazine and turned that publication into another voice for women's sexual freedom.

One year after *Sex and the Single Girl*, Betty Friedan's *Feminine Mystique* (another best seller) launched the modern feminist movement. By the end of the decade, the feminist movement (also called the women's movement or women's liberation movement) was in full force. In 1970 two well-known books expressed the ideas of that movement. One was *Sisterhood Is Powerful*, a collection of feminist writings edited by Robin Morgan. The other was Kate Millett's *Sexual Politics*, an attack on sexism in literature and society.

■ *STEAL THIS BOOK*

For hippies and other countercultural types, certain books were "must reads." In *Revolution for the Hell of It* (1968), hippie activist Abbie Hoffman chronicled his life as a figure in left-wing politics. Hoffman followed that up a few years later with *Steal This Book*, which included advice on everything from growing marijuana to living in a commune.

The most antiestablishment magazine of the 1960s was undoubtedly *Rolling Stone*. Founded by Jann Wenner in 1967, the magazine covered the new world of rock-and-roll music but also embraced left-wing politics. Many famous sixties journalists, such as Hunter S. Thompson, contributed articles to *Rolling Stone*.

The first issue of **ROLLING STONE** magazine featured a picture of Beatle John Lennon.

RESIDENTS OF THE DROP CITY COMMUNE in Colorado climb down from the top of their multisided geodesic dome home. The geodesic dome was designed by Buckminster Fuller in 1949 and became popular during the hippie movement of the 1960s.

CHAPTER SEVEN

POP!
ART AND DESIGN OF THE 1960s

After World War II, New York replaced Paris and war-torn Europe as the art capital of the world. Abstract expressionists such as Jackson Pollock dominated the scene. These artists filled their canvases with random paint splashes, marks, and drippings that seemed to map their turmoil and inner struggles.

But in the early 1960s, Americans turned away from the brooding introspection and anxiety of abstract expressionism. They wanted attractive and seductive images such as those they saw on TV. Fine art was no longer distant and remote. Art, popular culture, advertising, and mass media all joined together in the 1960s. In many ways, images became more important than words.

■ LOOKING TO THE FUTURE

In the late 1950s, two young artists from the South, Jasper Johns and Robert Rauschenberg, pointed out the future of U.S. art. Both had studied art at Black Mountain College in North Carolina. They moved to New York, where they worked in neighboring studios. In 1960 Johns made a bronze sculpture of two Ballantine Ale

81

ROBERT RAUSCHENBERG stands in front of his portrait of President John F. Kennedy in 1967. Rauschenberg helped set the stage for the pop art movement.

cans, painted to look just like the real things. What sort of art was this that used objects from a liquor store?

Meanwhile, Rauschenberg walked around the streets of New York picking up interesting things out of the garbage and the gutter. From all this junk, he made what he called combines, part sculpture and part painting. Rauschenberg's most famous combine, *Monogram*, featured a real, stuffed Angora goat with an automobile tire around its waist like a skirt. The work was eerie, funny, and frightening at the same time.

By the early sixties, Rauschenberg was making huge, mural-sized canvases. He filled them with enlarged photographs taken straight from the newspaper, silk-screened onto the canvas, and adorned by swipes and swabs of paint. His pieces looked like the competing, flickering, ever-changing images of channels switching on a TV set.

■ AMERICAN STUFF

Following Johns and Rauschenberg's lead, a number of other young artists, including David Hockney, Roy Lichtenstein, Claes Oldenburg, and Andy Warhol created a new art movement in the early 1960s. That movement was called pop—because it was based in popular culture. With great humor, pop art celebrated consumerism and mass production. The artwork incorporated everyday objects and images—cartoons, advertisements, and consumer products. It was colorful and fun.

Roy Lichtenstein was one of the earliest pop artists. His paintings were unmistakable—big blown-up panels taken straight from comic books. They were copies of copies that even included bubbles of dialogue and enlarged Benday dots, a shading technique used in commercial printing.

Another early pop artist, James Rosenquist, made some of the most powerful, image-filled paintings of the 1960s. *F-111*, made in 1964–1965, is 10 feet (3 meters) high and 80 feet (24 m) long. It includes aluminum panels with pictures of an F-111 fighter jet, a little girl's face, a Firestone tire, a pile of spaghetti, a lightbulb, and a nuclear mushroom cloud turning into a multicolored umbrella. The

[Pop art] incorporated everyday objects and images—cartoons, advertisements, and consumer products. It was colorful and fun.

work is bright and colorful. But it is also a dark commentary on U.S. military power and the growing conflict in Vietnam.

Roy Lichtenstein created *THINKING OF HIM* in 1963.

Pop spread fast, far, and wide. Claes Oldenburg used foam, fabric, and other materials to make "soft sculptures"—a couch-sized baked potato and a large, realistic hamburger. Wayne Thiebaud painted mass-produced desserts—cakes, pies, and sundaes—all lined up in a row.

Hands down, the most famous pop artist was Andy Warhol. Warhol *was* pop art. Ultracool, hip, and detached, Warhol became a celebrity himself. He was unmistakable with his white blond wig and distinctive horn-rimmed glasses. His *Campbell's Soup Cans*, perfectly realistic "portraits" of Campbell's Soup cans in thirty-two flavors, caused a sensation in 1962, as did his perfectly copied Brillo soap pad boxes set upon an art gallery floor a few years later. The great art of

ANDY WARHOL *(center)* created artwork out of brand-name products and media images.

Pop art pioneer Andy Warhol understood how mass media shapes our perceptions and how it can create a larger-than-life reality based on image and illusion. Warhol was born in Pittsburgh in 1928. His real name was Andrew Warhola. His parents were hardworking, Catholic immigrants from Eastern Europe. Andy was a sickly child, bedridden for long periods, and an outcast among his schoolmates. He was very close to his mother, Julia. While sick at home, young Andy would draw constantly, listen to the radio, and gather pictures of movie stars around his bed. He studied commercial art at Carnegie Mellon University in Pittsburgh, and in 1949, he moved to New York City. There, he changed his last name to Warhol and launched a successful career in magazine illustration and advertising. He became well known for his loose, whimsical ink drawings.

Warhol longed to be recognized as a fine artist. When he exhibited *Campbell's Soup Cans* in 1962, he got his wish. Overnight, he became the most famous artist in the United States. Warhol pretended not to care about his celebrity, saying that "in the future, everyone will be famous for 15 minutes." He called his art studio the Factory and said that he wanted to be a machine, since he thought art was a mechanical, unemotional process. He cut images out of newspapers and magazines. Then he used commercial printing techniques to reproduce the images over and over again, as if by an assembly line. He made prints of dollar bills, Coca-Cola bottles, and other products, as well as paintings of celebrities such as Elizabeth Taylor. Warhol, himself painfully shy and reclusive, surrounded himself with a cast of street people, partygoers, and sexy females. On June 3, 1968, a disturbed woman and studio hanger-on came into the Factory and shot Warhol five times. He was lucky to survive but was plagued by complications from the wounds for the rest of his life. For more than two decades, Warhol was at the center of New York art, fashion, and society. He socialized with Jackie Kennedy, Truman Capote, and other celebrities. Andy Warhol died unexpectedly, after undergoing surgery, on February 22, 1987.

85

the United States, said Warhol, was the "stuff" the country produced—standardized, brand-name products—always the same, immediately identifiable.

After film star and sex symbol Marilyn Monroe died in 1962, Warhol created a silk-screened reproduction of a photo of the actress set in a field of gold.

Monroe was a U.S. icon, and Warhol's painting resembled the Catholic icons he saw at church during his youth in Pittsburgh, Pennsylvania. Warhol's series of portraits of a grieving Jackie Kennedy after her husband's assassination was one of the most profound, universal expressions of the nation's grief at that time. And all Warhol did to create it was to make a screen print of a newspaper photograph.

nes Martin, and Donald Judd made art out of the simplest elements—cubes and straight lines. They argued that "less was more" and that simplicity was sublime.

Artists such as George Segal made "installation art," theatrical environments created with life-sized human figures and real objects. Christo, Yoko Ono, and Robert Smithson were "conceptual artists," whose works were made of ideas. They staged

" In the future, everyone will be famous for 15 minutes."

—Andy Warhol, 1968

Warhol named his New York art studio the Factory to emphasize the commercial, workmanlike nature of his process and the standardization of his "products." He gathered around him an entourage of unique characters from the fringes of New York society. The group began to make long movies in which nothing happened or simple random events went on in repetition.

■ FAR OUT

Anything went in the 1960s art world. Minimalists such as Frank Stella, Ag-

theatrical performances known as happenings. Happenings usually combined sculpture, dance, and music or sound, often with audience participation. Other artists made "Earth art" out of the land itself.

Op art (short for optical art) fit well with the playful, mind-altered mood of the 1960s. Op art is artwork that plays tricks on the eye. The often geometric images seem to swell, change, vibrate, flash, or reveal hidden objects when you look at them. Bridget Riley was among op art's most famous practitioners.

■ OTHER IMAGES

Romare Bearden worked in Harlem, New York City's main African American neighborhood, far from the fashionable world of pop and Warhol. Bearden created work that reflected the tensions, energy, and joys of the African American experience. As the civil rights struggle intensified, Bearden created strong social and political narratives using the technique of collage (a French word that means "gluing"). Bearden cut up photographs and glued them on a canvas in seemingly random order. His works—disjointed, jarring, and exciting—frequently showed images of life in Harlem.

The most famous female artist of the 1960s was Georgia O'Keeffe. She was nearing the end of a long career at the time. O'Keeffe had renounced the New York art world in the 1930s and moved to the tiny northern New Mexico town of Abiquiu. Her bold graphic images were out of vogue during the abstract expressionist years. But in the sixties, with the return of strong imagery and the rise of pop art, O'Keeffe's popularity rose. And with the rise of feminism in the United States, O'Keeffe became a hero to many women.

GEORGIA O'KEEFFE, standing with one of her paintings in the New Mexico desert, became a feminist icon in the 1960s.

A great many other female artists emerged in the 1960s. They included Louise Nevelson with her large "assemblages" (made from discarded furniture, scrap wood, and other everyday objects) and Helen Frankenthaler with her large canvases of stained color.

■ BUILDING WITH SKY AND SPACE

Before the 1960s, skyscrapers and boxy buildings were the norm in U.S. architecture. But like visual artists of the decade, architects of the 1960s experimented with new styles. Some created streamlined structures, accentuating motion and natural forms. Others, influenced by space travel and the race to the moon, made space-age, futuristic designs.

The work of Eero Saarinen seemed to sum up the new, architectural spirit of the age. With its free-flowing spaces and swelling, sail-like roofs, Saarinen's TWA Terminal at the John F. Kennedy Airport in New York (created between 1956 and 1963) looks like an enormous bird in flight. Saarinen's Gateway Arch in Saint Louis, Missouri, built in 1965, stands 630 feet (192 m) high. It frames the city like a giant stainless-steel rainbow. (Both the TWA Terminal and the

EERO SAARINEN designed the TWA Terminal at John F. Kennedy Airport in New York with curved ceilings and glass walls to give the feeling of flight.

Gateway Arch were completed after Saarinen's death in 1961.)

Buckminster Fuller was not just an architect. He was also an inventor, writer, scientist, and teacher. He made his most important contribution to architecture, the geodesic dome, in 1949. The dome was a strong, lightweight, multisided building. In the 1960s, young people discovered Fuller. They loved his geodesic dome—a simple structure that allowed people to live in harmony with nature. Some hippies, like those at the Drop City commune in Colorado, built geodesic domes to live in. Fuller was also an environmentalist. He advocated alternative energy systems, such as solar power and wind power. These ideas also made him even more popular among youth of the 1960s.

■ GOING MOD

In 1964 *Vogue* magazine showed readers the latest style from London. The creation of fashion designer Mary Quant, it was the miniskirt. It landed somewhere about 8 inches (20 centimeters) above the knee. No way am I wearing that, some older women said when they saw it in the magazine. But teenagers were another story. They loved the miniskirt and its sister outfit, the minidress. Miniskirts were sexy. Miniskirts were modern (shortened to *mod* in the 1960s). Miniskirts were the perfect clothing for the new, youth-centered 1960s. They looked terrific with tights and knee-high "go-go" boots.

But miniskirts and go-go boots were just the beginning of mod fashion. Young women dressed for the decade in big hoop earrings, big black sunglasses, big false eyelashes, wildly printed fabrics, stripes, sparkles, beads, you name it. Even young men got into the act with paisley print shirts, striped pants, and pointy boots.

Originating in London, the mod look wasn't the same as the hippie look. But after a while, the labels didn't matter. By the late 1960s, rules about fashion had changed dramatically. For men it was no longer taboo to dress in colorful clothing or wear long hair. Women didn't always have to wear modest skirts and dresses. They could wear jeans—even to work and school. The changes in fashion also helped blur the line between the sexes. Old people commonly remarked, "You can't tell the boys from the girls anymore."

89

The wife of President John F. Kennedy, Jackie Kennedy became a star in her own right. She was famous for her stunning good looks, her fashionable good taste, and the stoic way in which she handled her husband's death. She was born Jacqueline Lee Bouvier in 1929. Her parents were wealthy, and young Jackie lived a life of privilege. She attended private schools, rode horses, and traveled abroad. She graduated from George Washington University in 1951 and then took a job at the *Washington-Times Herald*. There, she wrote a daily "human interest" column, accompanied by her own photographs. In 1953 Bouvier married John Kennedy, who was then a U.S. senator. They had three children, one of whom died in infancy.

When Kennedy became president, his wife attracted just as much attention as he did. She wore a pink pillbox hat at her husband's inauguration. Immediately, she sparked a fashion trend—U.S. women rushed out to buy their own pillbox hats. Jackie's outfits—designed by Valentino, Givenchy, and official White House designer Oleg Cassini—were always the talk of the town. "Jackie introduced Middle America to that sophisticated look," explained twenty-first-century fashion designer Anna Sui. "She gave glamour in this country a European flavor." Even the French, famous for their fashion snobbery, looked on Jackie Kennedy with awe. She didn't limit her good taste to clothing. She renovated the White House during her husband's term, filling it with fine art, antiques, and custom furnishings. After her husband's death, Jackie continued setting fashion trends. In 1966 she showed off the latest in flat shoes. In 1967 she donned chain belts and oversized black sunglasses. Jackie married wealthy Greek businessman Aristotle Onassis in 1968—becoming Jackie Onassis and thereby attaining her most famous nickname, Jackie O. Jackie O was always the center of attention. She kept company with famous writers, artists, actors, and socialites. Photographers constantly tried to snap her picture. In 1978 she began working as an editor with the Doubleday publishing house in New York. She died of cancer in 1994.

JACKIE O in 1968

MARY QUANT *(FAR RIGHT)* **WAS AT THE FOREFRONT OF MOD FASHION** in the 1960s. Here she poses with models wearing her miniskirts and other designs.

■ GROOVY!

Suddenly, pop art and mod fashions were everywhere. Advertisers used peace symbols, flowers, and paisley to appeal to young buyers. Lava lamps were a hot item in the 1960s. The brightly colored, constantly changing lamps (filled with hot flowing wax) provided an otherworldly glow to many college dorm rooms. Album covers and posters for rock-and-roll shows featured some of the most compelling visual art of the 1960s. Lots of this artwork was psychedelic, with swirling colors and distorted images.

Product design went in new directions in the 1960s. Round red TV sets and egg-shaped chairs that hung from the ceiling were just a few of the eye-popping offerings. Colors were bright and bold. Ford Mustangs—incredibly popular small cars that debuted in 1964—came in many colors, including Ivy Green, Candyapple Red, Tahoe Turquoise, Acapulco Blue, and Playmate Pink.

THE BEVERLY HILLBILLIES—a popular TV show of the 1960s—placed a country family in the heart of the city for lots of laughs.

CHAPTER EIGHT

STAGECRAFT:
STAGE AND SCREEN IN THE 1960s

By 1960 televisions were commonplace in American homes. Three networks—ABC, NBC, and CBS—broadcast a variety of programming, including game shows, cartoons, situation comedies, adventure shows, sports, and news. Some shows offered lighthearted, even silly entertainment, which led one government official in 1961 to call television a "vast wasteland." But by then, more than 90 percent of U.S. homes had televisions. Regardless of the government official's opinion, Americans loved to watch TV.

Shows about family life had been popular in the 1950s, and that trend continued in the 1960s. *My Three Sons, The Dick Van Dyke Show,* and *The Andy Griffith Show* were just a few of a long list of heartwarming and comical 1960s family sitcoms.

TV writers of the 1960s knew that putting characters in unusual and unfamiliar situations was good for laughs.

The Beverly Hillbillies, for example, was a sidesplitting series about a backwoods family from Tennessee, resettled into posh society in Beverly Hills, California. *Gilligan's Island* told the story of a goofy group of castaways shipwrecked on a deserted island. And *Green Acres* reversed the *Beverly Hillbillies* scenario, placing a city-slicker husband and wife on a farm in the rural United States.

Well-loved children's favorites of the 1960s included the cartoons *Rocky and Bullwinkle, The Jetsons,* and *The Flintstones.* Americans of all ages watched *The Ed Sullivan Show.* This Sunday-night variety show had helped launch Elvis Presley's career in 1956 and was still going strong when the Beatles sang for Sullivan's nationwide audience in 1964. *Let's Make a Deal, The Newlywed Game,* and *Hollywood Squares* were popular game shows. *Dr. Kildare, The Fugitive,*

93

and *Ironside* were serious dramas about a young doctor, a man falsely accused of murder, and a wheelchair-bound detective, respectively. The soap operas *General Hospital* and *Days of Our Lives* were melodramatic, just as they are in modern times.

Some shows of the 1960s were downright preposterous. For instance, the star of *Mister Ed* was a talking horse. *Bewitched* followed the day-to-day struggles of a nice suburban family, most of whom were witches. And in *The Addams Family*, one cast member was creepier than the next—from the Frankenstein-like butler Lurch to the hair-covered Cousin It.

■ TIMELY TOPICS

The nightly TV lineup said a lot about U.S. culture and politics in the 1960s. People were focused on space exploration during that decade, so it's no surprise that many TV shows starred space travelers. *Lost in Space* was about a family shipwrecked in outer space, while *My Favorite Martian* told the story of a wacky Martian stranded on Earth. *Star Trek*, the wildly popular show that spawned many spin-off series and movies, followed the interstellar adventures of the starship *Enterprise* and its crew.

The Cold War was raging in the 1960s, and many TV programs featured spies and counterspies. *I Spy, The Man from UNCLE,* and *Mission Impossible* were all peopled by secret agents and international spy agencies. The sitcom *Get Smart* made fun of the other spy programs. The show's main character was Max Smart, also called Agent 86. He worked for a secret U.S. agency called CONTROL. The enemy agency was called KAOS. Every week, Agent 86 made trouble for KAOS with the help of high-tech gadgetry, including a handy shoe phone.

As the United States changed in the 1960s, it wasn't long before the counterculture arrived on television.

■ "SOCK IT TO ME"

As the United States changed in the 1960s, it wasn't long before the counterculture arrived on television. *The Mod Squad* debuted in 1968. *Mod* is another word for "hip," and the interracial Mod Squad was hip indeed.

It consisted of three young crime fighters: streetwise Michael, sexy Julie, and supercool Linc, who wore his hair Afro style. Being young and cool enabled the Mod Squad to work undercover and undetected among drug dealers and other criminals.

Perhaps the most famous show to embrace the counterculture was *Laugh-In*. This fast-paced variety show launched the careers of many well-known

THE STARS OF *LAUGH-IN* pose for a cast photo. The creators, Dan Rowan *(left)* and Dick Martin *(right)*, are seated at front.

"Sock it to *me*?"

—*Richard Nixon on* Laugh-In, *1968*

comedians, most notably Lily Tomlin and Goldie Hawn. *Laugh-In* (the name was a takeoff on "sit-in" and "be-in") was loaded with skits and zingy one-liners. The actors made lots of jokes about hippies, women's liberation, war protesters, and President Nixon. They recited goofy catchphrases such as "Sock it me" and "You bet your sweet bippy." In one of *Laugh-In*'s most memorial moments, Richard Nixon himself appeared on the show during his run for office in 1968. "Sock it to *me*?" he said awkwardly to the TV cameras. The appearance made the normally stiff Nixon look a little more human and lighthearted—and perhaps even contributed to his victory in the 1968 election.

◼ PERSUASION

During and between popular television shows of the 1960s, clever advertisements convinced viewers to buy everything from soap to green beans to cars. Recognizing television's power to influence as well as entertain, some people used it to send strong messages.

During the 1964 presidential race, for example, Lyndon Johnson's campaign produced a frightening TV commercial. The spot featured a pretty little girl counting the petals on a daisy. But then her countdown morphed into a countdown to a nuclear explosion. A giant mushroom cloud filled the screen. Johnson's ad was designed to scare viewers—and to convince them not to vote for his opponent, Barry Goldwater, who favored using nuclear weapons in Vietnam. Many people criticized Johnson for his scare tactics. His campaign pulled the ad after just one showing.

The long-running investigative news magazine *60 Minutes* debuted on CBS in 1968. This show and others attempted to do more than just amuse audiences. It also tried to expose wrongdoing, educate viewers, change public opinion, and perhaps change public policy.

"Peace, Little Girl"—known better as **THE DAISY SPOT** ad—created a controversy in 1964 by juxtaposing a little girl *(right)* counting with a nuclear countdown.

Television's power to change opinions was made very evident early in the 1960s. In September and October 1960, presidential candidates John F. Kennedy and Richard Nixon participated in a series of debates—the first televised presidential debates in history. A month before the first debate, Nixon was hospitalized with a knee injury. When he arrived at the debate, he was still underweight and pale. He also sported a "five o'clock shadow" on his face. In other words, he could have used a shave. Kennedy, in contrast, had spent the previous weeks campaigning in sunny California. In addition to his natural good looks, he was tan and well rested. Seventy million Americans tuned in for the first debate on September 26. The two candidates discussed domestic issues.

Afterward, most television viewers said that Kennedy had won the debate. People who listened on radio, on the other hand, gave the victory to Nixon. Why had Kennedy impressed the TV viewers more than the radio listeners? The answer was obvious: Kennedy looked better than Nixon did. In November, on Election Day, Kennedy beat Nixon at the polls. Did his good looks play a part in his victory? Based on the debates, it seems likely that they did. After the Kennedy–Nixon debates, politicians understood that they had to tailor their campaigns for the television age. It wasn't enough to be the smartest, the most articulate, or the most experienced—the winning candidate also had to look good on TV.

97

JOHN F. KENNEDY *(right)* looked better on TV than RICHARD NIXON *(left)*.

A new television station, PBS (the Public Broadcasting Service), formed in 1969. Its goal was to bring high-quality arts, educational, documentary, news, and children's shows to U.S. television. The puppet-filled *Sesame Street*, perhaps the most popular children's TV show of all time, was one of the first-ever PBS programs.

■ BIG SCREEN

Just like television, the motion picture industry produced a variety of different offerings in the 1960s—from full-length cartoons to musicals to serious dramas. And like television shows of the decade, many movies reflected trends in U.S. society. The Cold War featured big in many movies of the early

Big Bird and the cast of **SESAME STREET** appear on the set during shooting in 1969.

1960s. *The Manchurian Candidate* (1962), *Fail-Safe* (1964), and *Seven Days in May* (1964) examined U.S.–Soviet relations, Communism, and the threat of nuclear war. These films took the prospect of nuclear destruction very seriously and captured the public's fears and suspicions about Communism. *Dr. Strangelove or: How I Learned to Stop Worrying and Love the Bomb* (1964) did just the opposite. This dark comedy played nuclear war for laughs, no doubt shocking many Americans in the process.

There was no shortage of action and adventure movies in the 1960s. Some of them, especially *The Wild Bunch* (1969), displayed more violence than had previously been seen in U.S.

films. The James Bond series of films began in 1962 with *Dr. No* and with the handsome Sean Connery playing the lead role. Just like TV secret agents, the classy spy James Bond was a cold warrior—his adversaries were often Communist agents.

Some classic movie musicals appeared in the 1960s: the tragic *West Side Story* (1961), the cheerful *Music Man* (1962), and a children's favorite, *Mary Poppins* (1964). But far and away the most beloved was 1965's *The Sound of Music*, starring Julie Andrews as a spunky governess to seven musical Austrian children—all of whom must escape from Nazi soldiers at the film's end.

Julie Andrews sings in the Alps in the role of the governess Maria in *THE SOUND OF MUSIC*.

Patty Duke has had a long career in both television and film. Born in Elmhurst, New York, in 1946, she was a child star, appearing in commercials, movies, and TV shows. Her big break came in 1959, when she won the role of Helen Keller in the stage version of *The Miracle Worker*. Duke played the stage role for two years and then played the same part in the film version of *The Miracle Worker* in 1962. She won an Oscar as Best Supporting Actress for this role. At the age of sixteen, she was the youngest person ever to win an Oscar at that time. Patty Duke became a household name when she starred in her own sitcom, *The Patty Duke Show*, from 1963 to 1965. She played two roles—Patty Lane and her "identical cousin," Cathy Lane. Teenage Patty Lane was a typical American girl. She loved rock and roll and hot dogs, while Cathy, who came from Scotland, was more of a snob.

Duke left her girlhood roles for a more grown-up part in the film *Valley of the Dolls* in 1967. This cult favorite had Duke as a talented young singer who enjoys great success, until she gets addicted to prescription drugs. The movie featured lots of mod hairdos and minidresses, making it a classic sixties time capsule. Patty Duke's acting career continued successfully through the 1970s. She made headlines in 1982 when she revealed that she had manic-depressive illness. She became a spokesperson

PATTY DUKE played Neely O'Hara in 1967's *Valley of the Dolls*.

and advocate for others with the disease. Continuing work as an actress, she also served as president of the Screen Actors Guild from 1985 to 1988. Duke worked in both TV and films for the remainder of the twentieth century and has continued acting in the twenty-first century. She has also been active in political causes, such as the fight for nuclear disarmament.

In the mid-1960s, youth culture came to the movies just as it had to television. It started in 1964 with *A Hard Day's Night*, which starred the famous British singers the Beatles as themselves. Later in the decade, *Yellow Submarine* (1968), an animated movie, featured animated Beatles and lots of good Beatles songs.

Medium Cool, from 1969, was a fictional film. But it incorporated real-life footage of the protests outside the 1968 Democratic National Convention in Chicago. *Easy Rider*, also from 1969, told the tale of two hippies exploring the United States by motorcycle.

Several classic films of the 1960s weren't about hippies or peace protesters, but they did speak to the youthful urge to rebel during that decade. *Bonnie and Clyde*, released in 1967 and starring Warren Beatty and Faye Dunaway, was heavy on violence. The movie made crime and the outlaw life look glamorous—even when the attractive lead characters ended up riddled with bullets in the final scene. Also in 1967, *The Graduate* told of a young man (played by Dustin Hoffman) right out of college who rejected his parents' suburban lifestyle while at the same time carrying on a steamy affair with an older woman. (The film's soundtrack featuring the music of folk duo Simon and Garfunkel was also a big hit.) Finally, 1969's *Midnight Cowboy*, also starring Dustin Hoffman, examined the risqué side of life in New York City—including drug use and homosexuality.

Faye Dunaway and Warren Beatty in **BONNIE AND CLYDE**.

AMERICA IN THE 1960s

Some of the greatest films of the 1960s were the work of groundbreaking filmmaker Stanley Kubrick. Born in New York in 1928, Kubrick began his career as a photographer for *Look* magazine. He learned filmmaking on his own, with a rented camera. He made a few short documentary films in the early 1950s. In 1956 Kubrick moved to Hollywood to make movies with the major studios. His first big success was *Paths of Glory*, an antiwar-themed film set during World War I (1914–1918). He followed that up with *Spartacus* in 1960 and *Lolita* in 1962. In 1964 Kubrick produced *Dr. Strangelove or: How I Learned to Stop Worrying and Love the Bomb*. The movie sent a blunt message: War is absurd and military leaders are buffoons. Since the anti–Vietnam War movement was just getting started in 1964, the movie couldn't have been timelier. It earned Kubrick great acclaim, including several Oscar nominations. Kubrick's next film was *2001: A Space Odyssey*, made in 1968. This science-fiction movie was set in the future (2001), a time when—from the 1960s viewpoint—interplanetary space travel was going to be commonplace. The film featured stunning, balletic images of spacecraft in flight, accompanied by dramatic music. Mod space suits, podlike furniture, and psychedelic lights and colors completed the futuristic scene. Critics called *2001* a masterpiece, and Kubrick took home an Oscar for special effects for the film. In the following decades, Stanley Kubrick continued to make movies, including *Barry Lyndon* and *The Shining*. He died in 1999.

STANLEY KUBRICK *(right)* gives directions to the actors on the set of *2001: A Space Odyssey*.

■ "AGE OF AQUARIUS"

Those who were uncomfortable with the edgy movies of the late 1960s could still enjoy old-fashioned song and dance on Broadway. Broadway musicals, including *Bye Bye Birdie*, *The Fantasticks*, and *Mame*, were filled with catchy tunes and clever story lines. *Fiddler on the Roof* was somewhat more serious—dealing as it did with poor Jews struggling for survival in turn-of-the-nineteenth-century Russia. But it still offered rousing musical numbers and even some laughs. *Cabaret*, which takes place in Germany before World War II, had a dark, sophisticated edge with terrific song and dance numbers.

Broadway would never be the same, though, after *Hair* debuted there in 1968. *Hair* was about hippies, and its opening number, "[the Age of] Aquarius," introduced yet another name for the sixties counterculture. Not only did the play deal openly with sex and drug use, it also featured one scene in which most of the cast members take off all their clothes. Audiences in New York were ready for *Hair*, but some other cities refused to have it staged there.

Playwrights did not hesitate to take on controversial themes in the 1960s. *Who's Afraid of Virginia Woolf*, opening in 1962 and written

Playwrights did not hesitate to take on controversial themes in the 1960s.

by Edward Albee, explores the bitter, alcohol-drenched relationship between a college professor and his wife. *Boys in the Band* (1968) deals with homosexuality, a topic that made many people uncomfortable in the 1960s. *Blues for Mister Charlie* (1964), written by acclaimed novelist James Baldwin, examines racial hatred in a small southern town.

103

THE SHANGRI-LAS were a popular "girl group" of the 1960s.

CHAPTER NINE

"MY GENERATION":
MUSIC IN THE 1960s

Musically, the 1960s started off quietly. Elvis Presley came home after two years in the army. Earlier, in the 1950s, Presley had shocked audiences with his swiveling hips and raucous rock and roll. But in the spring of 1960, at a "Welcome Home Elvis" concert on television, audiences saw a much tamer Elvis Presley. He sang the romantic "Love Me Tender" and "Witchcraft" with crooner Frank Sinatra. Meanwhile, many of Presley's fellow rock-and-roll pioneers had died or gotten in trouble with the law.

Was rock and roll—with its electric instruments and heavy beat—on its way out? Many parents hoped so. The older generation preferred classic singers such as Judy Garland. Her 1963 comeback concert at Carnegie Hall in New York was a showstopper.

But record companies were much more interested in the youth market. Teenagers of the 1960s had money to spend on records, fan magazines, transistor radios, and concert tickets. Performers such as Lesley Gore and the Shangri-Las spoke to young females with songs about teen heartbreak and bad-news boyfriends. More upbeat, the five blond Beach Boys sang about surfing, fast cars, pretty girls, and Southern California. No, rock and roll was nowhere near gone. But it encompassed all sorts of new sounds and rhythms in the early 1960s.

DANCE CRAZY

Rock and roll was made for dancing—but not for slow dancing. In the 1960s, young people wanted to shake their hips—and every other part of their anatomy.

105

The 1960s dance craze began when a singer named Chubby Checker sang "The Twist" on the TV show *American Bandstand*. It was a song about a dance. And in case listeners needed some help with the steps, every record sold included these instructions: "Imagine you are stubbing out a cigarette with both feet whilst drying your back with a towel." With that, U.S. teenagers were off and twisting.

But the Twist was just the beginning. Soon teenagers were learning the Hitch Hike, the Watusi, the Mashed Potato, the Jerk, the Swim, and the Frug. In nightclubs the nation over, young people could be found wriggling and writhing to these and dozens of other new dances. You didn't even need a partner to dance the Swim or the Frug. You could dance solo, duo, or in one big group.

Eventually, as rock and roll became more free form in the late 1960s, dancing became more free form too.

The Motown sound was infectious. . . . Listeners couldn't get enough of its catchy lyrics, soaring harmonies, and bouncy rhythms.

People quit Twisting and Swimming and simply swayed to the music as it moved them.

■ HITSVILLE U.S.A

Like much of U.S. society, the music industry was mired in racial inequality in the early 1960s. For years, mainstream radio stations had refused to play "race music"—that is, music by African American artists. That began to change in the 1950s with the rise of popular rhythm and blues (R&B) groups. But whites still owned the big record labels. For the most part, black musicians worked for barebones wages while white promoters and managers reaped big profits from their hit songs.

A black songwriter named Berry Gordy Jr. would change that formula. Borrowing eight hundred dollars from his family, Gordy founded Tamla Records in Detroit, Michigan, in 1959. One year later, Gordy launched Motown Records—named for Detroit, "the Motor City." In 1960 Tamla released "Shop Around" by the Miracles (with lead singer Smokey Robinson). The song soon hit number one on the R&B charts. That same year, Gordy merged Tamla and Motown to create the Motown Record Corporation.

THE MIRACLES, with lead singer Smokey Robinson *(far right)*, recorded many hits for Motown Records in the early 1960s.

The hits kept coming: "Please, Mr. Postman" by the Marvelettes (1961), "Heat Wave" by Martha and the Vandellas (1963), and "Baby Love" by the Supremes (1964). The Motown sound was infectious. It had roots in soul, R&B, and gospel. Listeners couldn't get enough of its catchy lyrics, soaring harmonies, and bouncy rhythms.

Not only was Motown owned and operated by African Americans, it also brought fame and often fortune to its black recording artists. Marvin Gaye, Diana Ross, the Temptations, Stevie Wonder, the Spinners, the Four Tops, Gladys Knight and the Pips, and the Jackson Five all got their start at Motown's "Hitsville U.S.A." studios. The Motown sound appealed to white as well as black audiences. With music, Berry Gordy and Motown helped the nation further down the road of integration. Great music helped bridge the racial divide.

■ "TURN, TURN, TURN"

In July 1963, on a hot day in Greenwood, Mississippi, black farmers gathered for a voter registration drive. To rally the assembled farmers, three singers stood on the back of a flatbed truck. Guitars in hand, they led the crowd in an old protest song, "We Shall Overcome." As the three men sang, the crowd joined in heartily.

The three singers were Theodore Bikel, Pete Seeger, and Bob Dylan. On the East Coast, where they normally sang, the three were well-known folk musicians. Playing simple instruments such as guitars and banjos, they sang folk songs—songs about the lives of ordinary people. Some of the songs were hundreds of years old—nobody knew who had written them. Other songs were brand new, written by the singers themselves.

But at the rally in Greenwood, the folksingers were more than just performers. They were political activists. The men took turns singing. For his turn, Bob Dylan sang "Only a Pawn in Their Game." The song was about civil rights activist Medgar Evers, who had been shot outside his home earlier that summer. Dylan's song spoke of injustice and terror. But it also told the audience that if they stuck together, they could fight injustice and win.

Folk music was very popular in the 1960s. It was a time of protest, and folk musicians used their songs to fuel that protest. They sang about civil rights. They sang antiwar songs. They sang about the struggles of poor people and working people. They sang at coffeehouses, folk festivals, protest rallies, and concert halls. Millions of fans bought folk music records. Among the most famous folksingers of the era were Bob Dylan; Joan Baez; Peter, Paul and Mary; Phil Ochs; and Odetta.

BOB DYLAN SINGS WITH FELLOW FOLKSINGER JOAN BAEZ at a civil rights rally in Washington, D.C., in 1963.

t's impossible to examine the 1960s without examining Bob Dylan, the famous singer, songwriter, and guitar player. He broke down barriers not only in music but also in politics and popular culture. In fact, the 1960s were a decade of rebellion, in part because Bob Dylan inspired people to rebel. His original name was Robert Allen Zimmerman. He grew up in northern Minnesota. As a student at the University of Minnesota, he fell in love with traditional U.S. folk music. Leaving college after his freshman year and by then calling himself Bob Dylan, he headed to Greenwich Village in New York City, the epicenter of the folk music scene. Dylan's first album, *Bob Dylan* (1962), featured traditional folk, blues, and gospel songs. His next album, *The Freewheelin' Bob Dylan* (1963), included mostly his own compositions. "Oxford Town" told about murdered civil rights workers. "Blowin' in the Wind" questioned war and indifference. Suddenly, the world took notice.

Dylan had a raspy voice. He was short and skinny. But his songs were enormous. Haunting and poetic, they asked pressing political and social questions. Soon Dylan added his voice to the civil rights struggle. And he kept writing songs. Most famously, "The Times They Are a-Changin'" told the older generation to step aside—because young people were about to change the world. In 1965 Dylan shocked many folk music purists when he embraced electric guitar and a harder rock-and-roll sound. As the sixties wound down, Dylan continued to explore different musical styles, including rhythm and blues and country. By then a huge star, he delighted music lovers for the rest of the century and into the next. Over the years, the honors poured in. Dylan received a Grammy Lifetime Achievement Award, Kennedy Center Honors, and induction into the Rock and Roll Hall of Fame. In 2004 *Rolling Stone* magazine named Bob Dylan the second-greatest musical artist of all time, second only to the Beatles.

109

■ INVASION

In the early 1960s, radio was less than perfect. Transistor radios—the inexpensive, portable radios used by many teenagers—sounded tinny. Many recordings were monophonic—coming through just one channel. AM stations sometimes featured a lot of static along with the music. But no amount of static could disguise the excitement coming out of U.S. radios in early 1964. The signal might have been weak, but the sound was powerful. It was unlike anything else on the radio.

On the surface, it was just a simple song with sweet lyrics. But that sweet little song would change U.S. society forever. The song was "I Want to Hold Your Hand," and the singers were the Beatles.

The Beatles were four young men from Liverpool, England: John Lennon, Paul McCartney, George Harrison, and Ringo Starr. In the early 1960s, while young Americans were listening to folk songs, Motown, the Beach Boys, and other teen favorites, the Beatles were honing their rock-and-roll act. By 1963 they were number one in Great Britain. Then they hit the U.S. airwaves. When that happened, U.S. teenagers went crazy—they had to hear more of the Beatles.

On February 7, 1964, the Beatles got off a plane in New York for their first U.S. tour. They performed on the popular *Ed Sullivan Show* two days later. In the audience, teenage girls screamed and cried. Some even fainted. And why not? The four Beatles were young, talented, and good looking. They performed in stylish suits and sharp black boots. The two lead singers, John Lennon and Paul McCartney, delivered winning harmonies. Their songs, accompanied by drums and electric guitars, were catchy, upbeat, and romantic.

Perhaps most intriguing, the four young men wore their hair long (for the time), below their ears and with bangs hanging down their foreheads. The press

THE BEATLES perform live on *The Ed Sullivan Show* on February 9, 1964.

The Beatles followed "I Want to Hold Your Hand" with five more number one songs in 1964.

called them Mop Tops and the Fab (fabulous) Four. Boys wanted to look like the Beatles—they grew their hair long too. The teenage public couldn't get enough of their records. Crowds mobbed the Beatles everywhere they went. Beatlemania gripped the United States. The Beatles followed "I Want to Hold Your Hand" with five more number one songs in 1964. By 1966 the Beatles were "more popular than Jesus," according to John Lennon.

The Beatles opened up the musical floodgates. Soon after their U.S. debut, dozens more British bands took their acts to the United States. Labeled the British Invasion, they included the Who, the Rolling Stones, the Dave Clark Five, the Moody Blues, the Animals, and the Kinks. Many U.S. rock groups modeled themselves after the Beatles.

The early Beatles were sweet and lovable. But many of the new British bands delivered a rougher brand of rock and roll. Their lyrics were edgy and defiant. Their singers were brash and scruffy. The Who even ended some concerts by smashing their instruments onstage.

■ THE SUMMER OF LOVE

If you wanted to take the pulse of American youth in the late 1960s, all it took was a visit to the Monterey International Pop Festival in June 1967. This outdoor rock-and-roll show attracted hundreds of thousands of young people to Monterey, California. It also kicked off the so-called Summer of Love, a giant hippie gathering in nearby San Francisco. One attendee described the scene:

Monterey! Hippies everywhere! Bearded and long-haired guys and beautiful little hippie girls every where Man, we just knew we were in for the time of our lives. Volkswagen buses and old cars painted up with peace symbols and flowers all over them. One group was (living?) in a big old bus that was painted all psychedelic looking. People walking and hitchhiking everywhere with big backpacks. People wearing furs and skins and moccasins and beads and feathers and flowers.

111

The 1960s reached a musical peak in August 1969 with a three-day music festival in upstate New York. The Woodstock Music and Art Fair took place at a 600-acre (243-hectare) dairy farm in rural Bethel, New York. Concert promoters expected two hundred thousand attendees, but more than half a million hippies eventually arrived. The crowds were so large that traffic snarled for miles on the roads outside Bethel. Eventually, many people abandoned their vehicles and walked. Concertgoers pitched tents and settled in for the "three days of peace and music" promised by the promoters. They were not disappointed. Many of the major performers of the decade took the stage. They included Joan Baez, Janis Joplin, Sly and the Family Stone, the Grateful Dead, the Who, Jefferson Airplane, and Jimi Hendrix.

As might be expected, some performers addressed the pressing political issues of the day. Country Joe McDonald performed his "I-Feel-Like-I'm-Fixin'-to-Die Rag," a humorous look at the heavy topic of the draft and the Vietnam War. Jimi Hendrix offered a distorted, electrified version of "The Star-Spangled Banner"—not as a patriotic anthem but as a cynical comment on U.S. foreign policy. Rain fell, the food ran out, and toilets overflowed, but nothing could dampen the spirits that weekend. "Everyone needed other people's help, and everyone was ready to share what he had as many ways as it could be split up," explained one festivalgoer. "Everyone could feel the good vibrations." People who attended Woodstock knew they had been part of something special. A documentary film about the festival came out a year later. The music came out on record (and later CD). Songwriter Joni Mitchell wrote a song called "Woodstock" that spoke of the festival's magical good feeling. In the early 2000s, Woodstock remains a famous symbol of the love, hope, and idealism of the 1960s.

More than half a million people drove and walked to a dairy farm in Bethel, New York, to attend WOODSTOCK in 1969.

> **"Hippies everywhere! Bearded and long-haired guys and beautiful little hippie girls every where Man, we just knew we were in for the time of our lives."**

Monterey Pop festivalgoer, 1967

JIMI HENDRIX performs at the Monterey International Pop Festival in 1967.

As colorful as the concertgoers were, the performers were even more riveting. With her unkempt hair and soulful swagger, Janis Joplin belted out hard-edged R&B at the Monterey concert. The Who sang their defiant youth anthem, "My Generation," and then smashed their instruments onstage. Jimi Hendrix, with his big Afro hairdo and purple feather boa, set his guitar on fire. For the most part, the music was loud, fast, and electric. Some of it was psychedelic, with dreamy, surreal sounds and musical distortions. Other acts at the three-day festival included the folksy Byrds, the mellow Mamas and the Papas, and the hippie favorite Grateful Dead.

■ THE MAINSTREAM

Rock and roll had many critics. One observer condemned the Beatles for their "idiotic" hairdos and "melancholy wail." But by the mid-1960s, most parents realized that rock and roll was here to stay. Still, that didn't mean they had to like it—or listen to it. The older generation had its own favorites during the decade.

Henry Mancini was one favorite. He wrote old-fashioned crowd-pleasers such as "Moon River" and "The Days of Wine and Roses" (with lyrics by the renowned Johnny Mercer). These romantic songs had no coarse lyrics, driving rock beats, or political bite. And for many Americans, that was just fine.

Burt Bacharach was another popular choice. Bacharach wrote many hit songs, including "Raindrops Keep Falling on My Head" and "What the World Needs

114

Many country singers of the 1960s sang about patriotism, God, and traditional roles for men and women.

Now Is Love." He teamed up with singer Dionne Warwick to become a pop favorite in the 1960s.

Then there was Barbra Streisand. Rock and roll might have been loud, but Streisand was louder, with a voice that could tear the roof off an auditorium. Streisand sang show tunes, nightclub standards, and pop ballads. She also starred on Broadway and TV and in the movies. Similarly, Liza Minnelli—one of Judy Garland's daughters—found fame on both stage and screen with her explosive voice. Nancy Sinatra, Frank's daughter, might have been more famous for her miniskirts, puffed-up hairdo, and go-go boots than for her voice. But she was talented, and her song "These Boots Are Made for Walkin'" was a huge hit in 1966.

For the most conservative Americans, country music did not disappoint. Many country singers of the 1960s sang about patriotism, God, and traditional roles for men and women. Tammy Wynette's "Stand by Your Man" told women to stick by their husbands, through thick and thin, even when they cheated. Patsy Cline, Johnny Cash, and Loretta Lynn gave audiences old-school country fare—with songs about heartbreak, cheating spouses, and hard times. In a direct attack on the counterculture, Merle Haggard recorded "Okie from Muskogee" in 1969. With this song, Haggard snarled at drug users, young men with long hair, and war protesters. The lyrics also told listeners that small-town Americans, with their old-fashioned country values, were the true patriots.

JOHNNY CASH PERFORMS WITH JUNE CARTER in 1968. Unlike most other country singers of the 1960s, Johnny Cash spoke out against the Vietnam War.

f you wanted to hear first-class singing in the 1960s, one of the best acts to check out was Barbra Streisand. Streisand grew up in Brooklyn, New York. An honors student, she graduated from high school in 1959. She immediately jumped into show business, singing in nightclubs and acting in plays. In 1962 Streisand got her first break: a small part in *I Can Get It for You Wholesale*, a Broadway musical. When Streisand sang the goofy "Miss Marmelstein" in that show,

Singer, actress, and entertainer BARBRA STREISAND performs a concert in Central Park in New York in 1967.

115

the music industry took notice. Not only was Streisand a gifted comic actress, but she had an amazing voice. Columbia Records quickly signed her to a recording contract. Her first album, *The Barbra Streisand Album*, appeared in 1963. Filled with heartfelt numbers such as "Cry Me a River," the album soared to the top of the charts and snagged two Grammy Awards. Streisand returned to Broadway in 1964 with the lead role in *Funny Girl*, a musical based on the life of comedian Fannie Brice. The show was another hit, and Streisand's career was unstoppable. She put out album after album and appeared

in her own television specials. In 1968 Streisand again starred in *Funny Girl*— this time the movie version. Her performance won her an Oscar for Best Actress (shared with Katharine Hepburn after a tie vote). One year later, Streisand starred in another movie musical comedy, *Hello, Dolly!* As the 1960s turned to the 1970s, Barbra Streisand was hard at work making records, giving concerts, singing on television, and acting in movies. By the early 2000s, she had not let up the pace. By then she had more than sixty records to her name, along with Emmys, Grammys, and Golden Globes.

WILMA RUDOLPH stretches to win the gold
medal in the 100-meter dash during the 1960
Olympics in Rome, Italy.

CHAPTER TEN

"THE THRILL OF VICTORY":
SPORTS IN THE 1960s

Americans loved sports in the 1960s—just as they did in earlier decades. But one device made sports an even larger part of their lives than ever before. That device, of course, was television. Broadcasters had been televising sports such as baseball and football since TV's early days. But in the 1960s, they broadcast a greater variety of sports and showed sporting events more often.

In 1960 the Olympics were televised for the first time. The Winter Games took place in Squaw Valley, California, that year. In addition to the television audience, more than forty-seven thousand spectators arrived to watch the competition in person. Normally, Americans weren't dominant in the Winter Games, but U.S. figure skater Carol Heiss won a gold medal at Squaw Valley. And the U.S. hockey team beat the fierce Soviet squad 3–2 and then went on to win its first-ever gold medal.

The 1960 Summer Games, held in Rome, Italy, were even more exciting for Americans. A brash young American named Cassius Clay (later known as Muhammad Ali), competing in the light heavyweight division, won a gold medal in boxing. A runner named Wilma Rudolph won three gold medals in track and field. Both athletes electrified the crowds. Rudolph's story was particularly impressive, since she had earlier been crippled by a childhood illness.

The following year, 1961, ABC launched a weekend TV sports program, *ABC's Wide World of Sports*. The show broadcast athletic contests from around the world, including popular sports such as figure skating, gymnastics, skiing, and track and field.

Muhammad Ali began his career as Cassius Clay, a likable young boxer from Louisville, Kentucky. Clay first came to fame at the 1960 Olympic Games in Rome. There, the handsome eighteen-year-old won a gold medal. Clay attracted lots of press attention, not only with his athletic talent but also with his bravado and clever words. He called himself "the greatest" and made up poems. "To make America the greatest is my goal / So I beat the Russian, and I beat the Pole," he recited after the Olympics. In 1964 Clay beat Sonny Liston to become the heavyweight champion of the world. That same year, he joined the Nation of Islam and embraced the Black Power movement. He also took an Islamic name, Muhammad Ali. Cassius Clay was a "slave name," Ali explained, passed down from the days when his ancestors were slaves.

By the mid-1960s, the Vietnam War was in full swing. Ali spoke openly against the war. "Why should they ask me to put on a uniform and go ten thousand miles [16,000 km] from home and drop bombs and bullets on brown people in Vietnam while so-called Negro people in Louisville are treated like dogs," he stated. Immediately, the public turned against Ali. Journalists, elected officials, and others attacked him as unpatriotic. The army tried to induct him in 1967, but Ali refused to serve. As punishment, boxing officials stripped him of his title and

MUHAMMAD ALI enjoys the applause of the crowd after receiving his light heavyweight boxing gold medal at the 1960 Olympics.

barred him from fighting for three years. In 1971 Ali returned to boxing. In 1974 he regained the heavyweight title by knocking out George Foreman in a fight called the Rumble in the Jungle in Kinshasa, Zaire (modern Democratic Republic of Congo). He lost the title to Leon Spinks and then won it again by beating Spinks in 1978. Through good times and bad, Ali kept up the colorful patter that made him a fan favorite. In 1984 Ali was diagnosed with Parkinson's disease, a brain illness. Although retired from boxing, Ali remains a very public figure. At the 1996 Olympic Games in Atlanta, Georgia, Ali had the honor of lighting the Olympic Torch.

"Float like a butterfly, sting like a bee."

—Muhammad Ali chant, referring to his style of boxing, 1960s

But it also showcased lesser-known sports, such as curling, rodeo, surfing, and badminton. *Wide World of Sports* was most famous for its dramatic introduction, narrated by sportscaster Jim McKay. As clips of exciting sports moments played on screen, McKay said, "Spanning the globe to bring you the constant variety of sport . . . the thrill of victory . . . and the agony of defeat . . . the human drama of athletic competition . . . this is *ABC's Wide World of Sports*." The show aired on ABC for thirty-six years—making it one of the longest-running programs in TV history.

■ RECORD BREAKERS

Records are meant to be broken, and athletes of the 1960s certainly did their part in knocking down records and raising the bar for future athletes. Roger Maris was one such record breaker. Playing for the New York Yankees, Maris hit sixty-one home runs in 1961. That total broke Babe Ruth's record of sixty home runs set in 1927. Maris set his record over a 162-game season that year, compared to Ruth's 154-game season. For some fans, the longer season lessened Maris's achievement. Nevertheless, he held the official home-run record for thirty-seven years.

In 1962 professional basketball player Wilt "the Stilt" Chamberlain set a record that has never been broken. Playing for the Philadelphia 76ers, Chamberlain scored 100 points in a game against the New York Knicks. He totaled 4,029 points that year—for an average of 50.4 points per game. Standing seven foot one (2.2 meters), Chamberlain had a stellar fourteen-year run in pro basketball. But no matter how good he was, he always seemed to fall short of his on-court rival, Bill Russell of the champion Boston Celtics.

In 1968 the long jump record stood at 27 feet 4¾ inches (8.4 m). Jumping at the Summer Olympics in Mexico City, American Bob Beamon hoped to best that record, if only by a fraction of an inch. What Beamon did instead was almost unbelievable. He jumped 29 feet 2½ inches (8.9 m)—almost 22 inches (55 cm) over the existing record. When Beamon learned of the official measurement after his jump, he collapsed to the ground in joy and disbelief. His record stood for twenty-three years.

■ BIG BUSINESS

Professional sports expanded in the 1960s. Major League Baseball added eight new teams, for a total of twenty-four, and lengthened its season by eight games. No one team dominated baseball in the 1960s, but players such as pitcher Sandy Koufax and outfielders Hank Aaron, Willie Mays, and Mickey Mantle were heroes to many Americans. Koufax, a Jewish player, surprised many when he refused to pitch during the first game of the World Series in 1965. The game fell on Yom Kippur, the holiest day on the Jewish calendar. Some fans were impressed by Koufax's religious devotion. Others criticized him for not playing when the team needed him. But his team, the Los Angeles Dodgers, won the series anyway.

Golf soared in popularity during the 1960s, mostly because of one man—Arnold Palmer. Palmer won golf's Masters Tournament four times—in 1958, 1960, 1962, and 1964. He also won numerous other tournaments, including the U.S. Open and the British Open. Following in Palmer's footsteps, Jack Nicklaus took home trophies in every major tournament—the Masters, the U.S. Open, the British Open, and the Professional Golfers' Association (PGA) Championship—in the 1960s and beyond. In U.S. living rooms, viewers loved to watch televised golf tournaments on weekends. Inspired by Palmer, Nicklaus, and other golfers, many Americans took up the sport.

For businesspeople, it was obvious that big-name sports equaled big-time money. The money came not only from ticket sales but also from advertisers, who paid high fees to promote their products on television during games. Players, who had previously been poorly paid, started to cash in on the field and off. For instance, a handsome young quarterback named Joe Namath signed a record-high $427,000 contract with the

JACK NICKLAUS *(LEFT)* AND ARNOLD PALMER study a green during the 1969 Masters Tournament.

For businesspeople, it was obvious that big-name sports equaled big-time money. The money came not only from ticket sales but also from advertisers, who paid high fees to promote their products on television during games.

New York Jets in 1967. Namath went on to earn more money by starring in television commercials for shaving cream and even women's panty hose.

As sports became more popular, promoters looked for new ways to attract fans—and keep the money rolling in. One development was the domed, or covered, stadium. When teams played inside a dome, it didn't matter whether it was raining or snowing outside—the game could always go on. And spectators could enjoy the game in heated or air-conditioned comfort.

The first domed stadium in the United States was the Astrodome in Houston, Texas. Home to the Oilers football team and the Astros baseball team, the dome opened in 1966. On the ground, where grass would normally be, a new substance called AstroTurf covered the playing surface.

Professional football was not going to be left behind in the sports explosion of the 1960s. The professional game had two leagues—the National Football League (NFL; dating to 1920) and the American Football League (AFL; formed in 1960). An intense rivalry developed between the two. To exploit this rivalry, league officials devised the idea of a championship game, with the leagues' top teams playing one another for the title of world champion. College football fans were familiar with postseason "bowl games," sometimes played in bowl-shaped stadiums. Picking up on this concept, AFL and NFL officials called their world championship the Super Bowl.

The first Super Bowl, Super Bowl I, took place on January 15, 1967. Tickets cost twelve dollars apiece, and almost sixty-two thousand fans attended the game at the Los Angeles Coliseum in California. Millions more watched on TV at home. The contest pitted the NFL's Green Bay Packers against the AFL's Kansas City Chiefs. The Packers were an easy winner, with a 35–10 final score. Bart Starr, the Packers'

Green Bay quarterback Bart Starr prepares to throw the football **DURING SUPER BOWL I** at the Los Angeles Coliseum on January 15, 1967.

veteran quarterback, was the game's most valuable player. After the successful first year, the Super Bowl got increasingly more popular—with more money in ticket sales, TV contracts, and advertising revenues.

■ BREAKING BARRIERS

On March 19, 1966, two basketball teams took to the court for the National Collegiate Athletic Association (NCAA) championship game. Like all basketball players of the time, they wore thin canvas sneakers, sleeveless jerseys, and supershort shorts. One team looked very much like most other college basketball teams of the era. The five starting players were wiry young white men, students at the University of Kentucky. It was the other team that turned heads. All five starting players—students from the Texas Western College—were African American. No major college team had ever started five black players in an NCAA championship game.

Texas Western coach Don Haskins didn't care what color his players were—he wanted to win. That's why he recruited the best ballplayers he could find—black and white—for his program at Texas Western. Kentucky coach Adolph Rupp, on the other hand, recruited only white players for his team. In fact, the whole Southeastern Conference (SEC), to which Kentucky belonged, was segregated. African Americans couldn't play on SEC teams.

Rupp made no secret of his dislike for his opponents. He said that Haskins's players were street toughs, recruited illegally to win a championship. Rupp also vowed that five blacks would never beat his white players. Fired up by Rupp's rude comments, the five Texas Western players dominated the court that night. They beat number one Kentucky 72–65 to become NCAA champions.

TEXAS WESTERN'S victory over Kentucky in March 1966 signaled the end of racial segregation in college basketball.

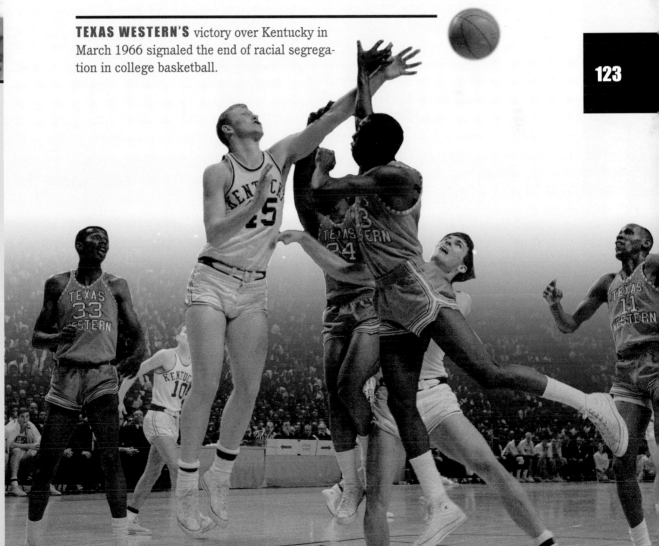

But more important than that victory, Texas Western changed college sports that night. Across the nation, segregation was coming to an end in schools, businesses, and other public places. And it finally came to an end in college athletics too. Attentive to Texas Western's victory, major U.S. universities began to recruit African American athletes. By the 1966–1967 season, even the SEC had integrated its basketball teams.

Professional sports had integrated much earlier. Particularly big-league baseball and basketball had black stars by the early 1960s—although even the most popular faced racial slurs from fans, opponents, and others. The Boston Celtics won the NBA championship nine years out of ten in the 1960s. The team included both black and white stars, including Bill Russell and Bob Cousy. Latin players joined U.S. baseball teams in the 1960s and made a big impact. Juan Marichal (Dominican) and Orlando Cepeda (Puerto Rican) of the San Francisco Giants and Roberto Clemente (Puerto Rican) of the Pittsburgh Pirates were big stars.

Golf and tennis were by far more segregated in the 1960s. Country clubs, where golfers and tennis players often honed their skills, were usually open to whites only. Golf and tennis were seen as "white sports," which few blacks had a chance to even try. Nevertheless, a few African Americans managed to break through to the pro ranks. In 1962

Golf and tennis were seen as "white sports," which few blacks had a chance to even try. Nevertheless, a few African Americans managed to break through to the pro ranks.

Charlie Sifford became the first African American on the PGA tour. In 1968 tennis player Arthur Ashe became the first African American to win the U.S. Open.

■ WOMEN WARRIORS

For female athletes, opportunities were limited in the 1960s. High schools and universities spent most of their sports budgets on men's teams. Men's college sports became big business in the 1960s, while women's teams sometimes resorted to bake sales and other fund-raisers to pay for uniforms, travel, and equipment.

O n October 16, 1968, two black U.S. athletes stood on the medal stand at the Summer Olympics in Mexico City. One athlete, Tommie Smith, had just won the gold medal in the 200-meter sprint. The other, John Carlos, had won the bronze in the same event. The silver medalist, Peter Norman of Australia, joined them on the medal stand. As the U.S. national anthem began to play and the U.S. flag rose to honor the gold medal winner, Smith and Carlos bowed their heads and raised their fists in the air. Smith wore a black glove on his right hand. Carlos wore the matching glove on his left. Neither Smith nor Carlos wore shoes. What was going on here?

TOMMIE SMITH (CENTER) AND JOHN CARLOS (RIGHT) give the Black Power salute in protest during the playing of the "Star-Spangled Banner" at the 1968 Olympics.

125

Smith and Carlos, students at San Jose State University in California, were members of the Olympic Project for Human Rights (OPHR). Originally, the organization wanted all African American athletes to boycott the 1968 Olympic Games, as a way to protest continued racial discrimination. The boycott never took place, but Smith and Carlos still wanted to make a statement at the Olympics. Their raised fists on the medal stand stood for Black Power. Their shoeless feet represented black poverty. Avery Brundage, head of the U.S. Olympic Committee, was outraged by the protest. He had Smith and Carlos stripped of their Olympic medals and expelled from the Olympic Village.

Brundage explained that the men's gesture had violated a basic Olympic principle— that the Olympic Games be nonpolitical. But many athletes supported the protesters. Peter Norman showed his solidarity by wearing an OPHR badge during the medal ceremony. The all-white U.S. Olympic crew team issued a statement of support. The all-black U.S. women's 4 x 100 relay team dedicated its gold medal to Smith and Carlos. A photograph of the two men, fists raised in the air, became a lasting image from the 1968 Olympic Games. After the controversy died down, Smith and Carlos went on to win many honors for their activism that day. They also both went on to coach high school track.

On April 19, 1967, Kathrine Switzer, a twenty-year-old Syracuse University junior, showed up to run the Boston Marathon. She had entered the famous 26-mile (42 km) race according to normal procedures. On her entry form, she listed herself as K. Switzer. Race officials assumed that K. Switzer was a man. After all, the Boston Marathon was for men only. Officials assigned Switzer a number, printed on a sheet of paper. Her college running coach picked up the number for her before the race started. Switzer pinned the number on her sweatshirt and began the race like all the others. She ran alongside her coach, Arnie Briggs, and her boyfriend, Tom Miller. All went well for the first 3 miles (5 km). Then news photographers noticed a woman running with a number pinned to her shirt. Women had run the Boston Marathon before—but not as official competitors with numbers. Then a race official named Jack Semple spotted Switzer. He jumped off the press truck and tried to pull her off the course. "Get the hell out of my race and give me that number," he shouted. Tom Miller shoved Semple aside. Semple returned to the truck, but he kept yelling. "You're in deep trouble," he told Switzer. Despite being officially disqualified, Switzer finished the race about four hours later. The next day, the incident—along with photos— was all over the papers. To many women,

Switzer was a hero. She had broken a barrier for women in sports, and she inspired them to take up running. Switzer went on to run thirty-five more marathons, including eight more Boston Marathons (which retained its ban on women until 1972). She won the New York City Marathon in 1974.

Race official JACK SEMPLE TRIES TO PULL KATHRINE SWITZER off the road at the 1967 Boston Marathon. Other runners came to her aid, and she finished the race.

1960s

AMERICA IN THE

When girls showed an interest in sports in the 1960s, parents and teachers often steered them toward "ladylike" sports such as synchronized swimming and figure skating. Peggy Fleming followed the figure skating path to the highest amateur level—an Olympic gold medal in 1968. Later, she skated professionally and worked as a sportscaster.

But for other female athletes, opportunities were few. After her three gold medals at the 1960 Olympics in Rome, Wilma Rudolph found few options for a career in sports. She drifted from job to job, teaching school and coaching young athletes. But she never made a living as a professional athlete.

Tennis player Billie Jean King was one of the few women who did manage to earn her living through sports. Born in California, she won her first U.S. National Championship in 1967 and won Wimbledon (the British championship) in 1966, 1967, and 1968. King was a leader off the court too. She fought for higher prize money for female tennis players and organized the Women's Tennis Association in the early 1970s. She continued to play—and win—throughout the 1970s and 1980s. She then turned to coaching.

BILLIE JEAN KING chases down the ball during the 1964 Wimbledon semifinals in England.

DEMONSTRATORS gather opposite the Lincoln Memorial in 1967 to protest the war in Vietnam.

FOREVER AFTER

I f there was only one word to describe the 1960s in the United States, that word would be *change*. Almost everything changed in the 1960s. Music, literature, clothing, politics, family life, race relations, and sexual attitudes—all of this changed radically.

Before the 1960s, women had few job choices. Most worked as wives and mothers. After the 1960s, women worked alongside men in all fields and professions. Before the 1960s, most Americans were afraid to openly criticize the government. After the 1960s, people routinely protested against government policies. Before the 1960s, most gay people hid their sexual orientation. After the 1960s, people came out of the closet in large numbers. Before the 1960s, black Americans often couldn't eat in the same restaurants as whites. After the 1960s, restaurants, hotels, schools, public transportation, and other institutions were open to people of all races.

People fought hard for these changes. Civil rights marchers endured beatings, bombings, and hateful words. Women faced ridicule when they demanded equal rights with men. War protesters were often beaten and hauled off to jail. Some were even shot. But people kept working for change. They envisioned a fairer, more peaceful, and more just world—and eventually their protests paid off.

129

No matter what their political persuasion, everyone who lived though the 1960s will likely agree—it was a time like no other. And after it was over, the United States would never be the same.

Although *change* might be the best word to describe the 1960s, other words apply. These words include *hope*, *idealism*, *freedom*, *youth*, and *creativity*. People wanted to "do their own thing" in the 1960s. Young people led the movement to create a counter-culture—an alternative to the old, conservative order. "From the very beginning, and President Kennedy's call to 'ask what you can do for your country,' it was a time when each person had a very real feeling that the individual could make a difference and make society and the world a better place. And it was a feeling that only got stronger as the sixties went on," recalls one baby boomer.

Did the 1960s make the world a better place? Yes and no. The young protesters of the 1960s were determined to stop the Vietnam War. But that war continued until 1975. Young voters wanted to send liberal politicians with new ideas to Washington. But Richard Nixon's "forgotten Americans" had other ideas. Nixon and his Republicans held onto power until the Watergate scandal forced Nixon from office in 1974. Ralph Nader and his Raiders wanted to clean up big business and the environment. They made great strides in the 1960s. But

in the coming decades, big corporations fought back, weakening many of the new rules and regulations. Hippies wanted to dress as they pleased, live off the land, and experiment with drugs. But eventually, they also had bills to pay, and many of them settled into traditional jobs, suburban neighborhoods, and family life. Some black radicals wanted to create a revolution in the United States. But law enforcement pushed back, and radicals had to settle for the legal gains of the civil rights movement.

Along with hope and idealism, the 1960s brought pain and tragedy. The killings of John F. Kennedy, Martin Luther King Jr., and Robert Kennedy were wrenching reminders that not everyone shared the vision of a new, peaceful, more just country. By the time the Vietnam War was over, almost sixty thousand Americans had been killed. Had they died for nothing? Many people thought so.

Despite the pain and protest, the 1960s also bathed the United States in a wave of good feelings. The Beatles, Woodstock, flower power, pop art, Jackie O, *Laugh-In*, and a man on the moon—these are the sights and sounds that many remember when they think of the 1960s. They recall a decade full of excitement, exploration, and experimentation. Youth and beauty were in. You could wear wild, colorful clothing, grow your hair long, and dance to rock-and-roll music.

In the first decade of the 2000s, more than half of all Americans were born after the 1960s ended. These Americans get their ideas about the 1960s from books, movies, music, and television. But learning secondhand about a time period is never the same as living through it. No matter what their political persuasion, everyone who lived though the 1960s will likely agree—it was a time like no other. And after it was over, the United States would never be the same.

The Beatles inspired tears of ecstasy in **AMERICAN TEENAGERS IN THE 1960S**. These girls are at a Beatles concert in New York.

1960
- John F. Kennedy and Richard Nixon take part in the first televised presidential debates.
- African American students in North Carolina begin a sit-in movement to desegregate stores and restaurants in the South.
- The Searle pharmaceutical company begins to sell birth control pills.
- Berry Gordy founds Motown Records.
- Cassius Clay (Muhammed Ali) and Wilma Rudolph win gold medals at the Summer Olympics in Rome.

1961
- John F. Kennedy creates the Peace Corps.
- The Bay of Pigs invasion fails in Cuba.
- Freedom Riders protest segregation at bus stations in the South.
- Roger Maris breaks Babe Ruth's home-run record.

1962
- The United States and the Soviet Union negotiate for the removal of nuclear missiles from Cuba.
- Consumers buy the first color televisions.
- Rachel Carson publishes *Silent Spring*.
- Helen Gurley Brown publishes *Sex and the Single Girl*.
- Andy Warhol exhibits his *Campbell's Soup Cans*.
- Wilt Chamberlain scores one hundred points in a professional basketball game.

1963
- Lee Harvey Oswald assassinates President John F. Kennedy.
- More than 250,000 people attend the March on Washington for Jobs and Freedom, where Martin Luther King Jr. gives his "I have a dream" speech.
- Betty Friedan publishes *The Feminine Mystique*.

1964
- Congress passes the Tonkin Gulf Resolution authorizing President Lyndon Johnson to use military force in Vietnam.
- Volunteers work to register black voters during Mississippi Freedom Summer.
- Klansmen kill three civil rights workers near Philadelphia, Mississippi.
- President Lyndon Johnson describes his vision of a Great Society.
- *Vogue* magazine introduces miniskirts to the U.S. public.
- *Dr. Strangelove* appears in movie theaters.
- The Beatles sing on *The Ed Sullivan Show*.
- Cassius Clay beats Sonny Liston to become the heavyweight champion of the world.

1965

- The first U.S. ground forces arrive in Vietnam.
- President Johnson declares a "War on Poverty."
- State troopers attack civil rights marchers in Selma, Alabama.
- Riots break out in the Watts neighborhood of Los Angeles.
- Mexican American farmworkers launch a consumer grape boycott.
- Ralph Nader publishes *Unsafe at Any Speed*.

1966

- The Student Nonviolent Coordinating Committee (SNCC) embraces the philosophy of Black Power.
- Huey Newton and Bobby Seale form the Black Panther Party.
- Betty Friedan and other feminists create the National Organization for Women.

1967

- Antiwar protesters hold a major rally in Washington, D.C.
- Amana introduces the first home microwave oven.
- Hippies attend the Human Be-In and the Summer of Love in San Francisco.
- *Rolling Stone* magazine begins publication.
- The Green Bay Packers and the Kansas City Chiefs play in Super Bowl I.
- Muhammad Ali refuses to be inducted into the U.S. Army.

1968

- Sirhan Sirhan assassinates Robert F. Kennedy.
- Protesters clash with police and the National Guard outside the Democratic National Convention in Chicago, Illinois.
- James Earl Ray assassinates Martin Luther King Jr.
- Robin Morgan organizes a protest at the Miss America Pageant.
- Richard Nixon appears on *Laugh-In*.
- *Hair* debuts on Broadway.
- Tommie Smith and John Carlos give the Black Power salute on the medal stand at the 1968 Summer Olympics in Rome.

1969

- Protesters across the United States hold the Moratorium to End the War in Vietnam.
- Neil Armstrong becomes the first human to walk on the moon.
- Gay New Yorkers riot outside the Stonewall Inn.
- More than half a million hippies attend the Woodstock music festival in upstate New York.
- Reporter Seymour Hersh breaks the story of the My Lai massacre in South Vietnam.
- The Public Broadcasting Service (PBS) launches *Sesame Street* on television.

10 Terry H. Anderson, *The Movement and the Sixties: Protest in America from Greensboro to Wounded Knee* (New York: Oxford University Press, 1995), 59.

11 Lorraine Glennon, ed., *Our Times: The Illustrated History of the 20th Century* (Atlanta: Turner Publishing,1995), 452.

11 Anderson, *The Movement and the Sixties*, 59.

11 Ibid., 59, 60.

13 Mark Hamilton Lytle, *America's Uncivil Wars: The Sixties Era from Elvis to the Fall of Richard Nixon* (New York: Oxford University Press, 2006), 115.

14 Nellie Connally and Mickey Herskowitz, *From Love Field: Our Final Hours with President John F. Kennedy* (New York: Rugged Land, 2003), 7.

15 CNN, "J.F.K. Assassination: Your Memories." *CNN.com*, November 22, 2003, http://www.cnn.com/2003/US/11/19/ys.jfk.1/index.html (September 11, 2007).

17–18 Harry Maurer, *Strange Ground: Americans in Vietnam 1945–1975, an Oral History* (New York: Henry Holt and Company, 1989), 152–153.

21 Enouch Pratt Free Library, "Fire and Faith: The Catonsville Nine File," *Enoch Pratt Free Library*, 2005, http://c9.mdch.org/page.cfm?ID=3 (September 11, 2007).

24 Todd Gitlin, *The Sixties: Years of Hope, Days of Rage* (New York: Bantam Books, 1987), 300.

24 Lytle, *America's Uncivil Wars*, 250.

26 Anderson, *Movement and the Sixties*, 208.

27 Lytle, *America's Uncivil Wars*, 257.

29 Anderson, *Movement and the Sixties*, 43.

30 Howard Zinn, *SNCC: The New Abolitionists* (Boston: Beacon Press, 1964), 23–24.

31 Sanford Wexler, *The Civil Rights Movement: An Eyewitness History* (New York: Facts on File, 1993), 115.

31 Ibid.

34 Ibid., 189.

35 Ibid., 208.

35 Ibid.

37 Ibid., 245.

39 Democracy Now! "On the 41st Anniversary of the Assassination of Malcolm X, 'The Ballot or the Bullet,'" *democracynow.org*, February 21, 2006, http://www.democracynow.org/article.pl?sid=06/02/21/1442222 (September 11, 2007).

41 Anderson, *Movement and the Sixties*, 169.

45 CNN, "Man on the Moon: Kennedy Speech Ignited the Dream," *CNN.com*, 2003, http://archives.cnn.com/2001/TECH/space/05/25/kennedy.moon/ (September 11, 2007).

46 Ibid.

46 Glennon, *Our Times*, 500.

47 Australian Broadcasting Corporation, "That Photograph," *abc.net*, 1999, http://www.abc.net.au/science/moon/earthrise.htm (September 11, 2007).

55 Robert F. Kennedy Memorial, "Life and Vision," *rfkmemorial.org*, n.d., http://www.rfkmemorial.org/lifevision/biography/ (September 11, 2007).

56 CNN, "LBJ's Great Society Speech," *CNN.com*, n.d., http://www.cnn.com/SPECIALS/cold.war/episodes/13/documents/lbj/ (September 11, 2007).

59 Anderson, *Movement and the Sixties*, 311.

59–60 Betty Friedan, *The Feminine Mystique* (1963; repr., New York: W. W. Norton & Company, 2001), 15.

64 Ralph Keyes, "Why We Misquote," *Ralph Keyes*, June 22, 2007, http://www.ralphkeyes.com/pages/books/niceguys/excerpt.htm (September 11, 2007).

65 Ibid.

65 Anderson, *Movement and the Sixties*, 282.

65 Biography Base, "George Wallace Biography," *Biography Base*, 2004, http://www.biographybase.com/biography/Wallace_George.html (September 11, 2007).

61 Lytle, *America's Uncivil Wars*, 269.

73 Tom Wolfe, "There goes (VAROOM! VAROOM!) that Kandy Kolored (THPHHHHHH!) tangerine-flake streamline baby (RAHGHHHH!) around the bend (BRUMMMMMMMMMMMMMMMM)," *Esquire*, November 1963.

85 Glennon, *Our Times*, 461.

90 Robert Haskell and Jessica Kerwin, "Fascinating Jackie," *Style.com*, 2007, http://

www.style.com/w/feat_story/041501/full_page.html (September 11, 2007).

96 Richard Nixon, quoting a catchphrase of *Laugh-In*, during a cameo appearance, broadcast on NBC, September 16, 1968.

106 SixtiesCity, "Dance Crazes of the Sixties," *Sixties City*, 2007, http://www.sixtiescity.com/Culture/dance.shtm (September 11, 2007).

111 Mark Sullivan, "'More Popular Than Jesus': The Beatles and the Religious Far Right," *Popular Music 6*, no. 3 (October 1987):313.

111 Lytle, *America's Uncivil Wars*, 220.

112 Anderson, *Movement and the Sixties*, 278.

113 Lytle, *America's Uncivil Wars*, 220.

113 Ibid., 146.

118 David Remnick, *King of the World: Muhammad Ali and the Rise of an American Hero* (New York: Random House, 1998), 105.

118 Ibid., 289.

119 Muhammad Ali, catchphrase, available online at "QuestDB," *QuoteDB.com*, January 8, 2008, http:www.quotedb.com/quotes/3980 (January 8, 2008).

119 IMDb, "ABC's Wide World of Sports," *Internet Movie Database*, 2007, http://www.imdb.com/title/tt0190895/ (September 11, 2001).

126 Kathrine Switzer, "The 1967 Boston Marathon," *Kathrine Switzer Home Page*, 2002, http://www.katherineswitzer.com/boston.html (September 11, 2007).

130 Julian J. Lewis, interview with author, June 7, 2007.

SELECTED BIBLIOGRAPHY

Anderson, Terry H. *The Movement and the Sixties: Protest in America from Greensboro to Wounded Knee*. New York: Oxford University Press, 1995.
Beginning with the Greensboro, North Carolina, sit-ins in 1960, this comprehensive book explores social and political activism in the 1960s.

Connally, Nellie, and Mickey Herskowitz. *From Love Field: Our Final Hours with President John F. Kennedy*. New York: Rugged Land, 2003.
Nellie Connally was with John F. Kennedy when he was assassinated. In this book, she reflects on her time with the Kennedys in Texas and the terrible events of November 22, 1963.

The Fog of War. DVD. Culver City, CA: Sony Pictures Classics, 2004.
In this Oscar-winning documentary, former secretary of defense Robert McNamara discusses his life and work. He offers insights into the Johnson and Kennedy administrations, the Vietnam War, and his own role in the conflict.

Friedan, Betty. *The Feminine Mystique*. 1963. Reprint, New York: W. W. Norton & Company, 2001.
Friedan's groundbreaking book is credited with igniting the feminist movement of the 1960s. Here, Friedan explains why women want more out of life than marriage and motherhood.

Gershon Gottlieb, Sherry. *Hell No, We Won't Go! Resisting the Draft during the Vietnam War*. New York: Viking, 1991.
The author interviewed dozens of men who were draft age during the Vietnam War. They told stories of why they refused to serve in Vietnam and how they resisted the draft. Interviewees include actor Richard Dreyfuss and boxer Muhammad Ali.

Gitlin, Todd. *The Sixties: Years of Hope, Days of Rage*. New York: Bantam Books, 1987.
Gitlin was Students for a Democratic Society (SDS) president and anti–Vietnam War leader. He tells the story of activism in the 1960s from a personal perspective.

Glennon, Lorraine, ed. *Our Times: The Illustrated History of the 20th Century*. Atlanta: Turner Publishing, 1995.
This lushly illustrated title offers a decade-by-decade and year-by-year survey of the twentieth century. It examines international happenings as well as cultural, political, and social milestones in the United States.

King, Martin Luther, Jr. *I Have a Dream: Writings and Speeches That Changed the World*. Edited by James M. Washington. San Francisco: Harper San Francisco, 1992.
Martin Luther King Jr. changed history with the power of his words. This collection includes King's most famous writings and speeches, including "Letter from a Birmingham Jail" and his "I have a dream" speech.

Lytle, Mark Hamilton. *America's Uncivil Wars: The Sixties Era from Elvis to the Fall of Richard Nixon*. New York: Oxford University Press, 2006.
Lytle examines the forces that disrupted and transformed U.S. society during the 1960s—from the civil rights movement and the antiwar movement to rock and roll and women's liberation.

Maurer, Harry. *Strange Ground: Americans in Vietnam 1945–1975, an Oral History*. New York: Henry Holt and Company, 1989.
Maurer interviewed U.S. soldiers, officers, nurses, reporters, and others who worked in Vietnam during three decades of U.S. involvement there. Their stories capture the reality and brutality of the Vietnam conflict.

Remnick, David. *Kings of the World: Muhammad Ali and the Rise of an American Hero*. New York: Random House, 1998.
Muhammad Ali was one of the most colorful and controversial characters of the 1960s. Remnick takes an intimate look at his athletic and political life during that decade.

Welsh, Douglas. *The History of the Vietnam War*. New York: Exeter Books, 1984.
This book offers a military history of the Vietnam War. Dramatic black-and-white photos show terrifying scenes of warfare.

Wexler, Sanford. *The Civil Rights Movement: An Eyewitness History*. New York: Facts on File, 1993.
This title tracks the key events of the struggle for African American civil rights. It features extensive quotes from politicians, reporters, civil rights leaders, and rank-and-file civil rights marchers.

Zinn, Howard. *SNCC: The New Abolitionists*. Boston: Beacon Press, 1964.
SNCC—the Student Nonviolent Coordinating Committee—was formed during the 1960 sit-in movement. Its college-student members quickly became leaders in the fight for civil rights. This book examines their struggles and successes.

Books

Anderson, Catherine Corley. *John F. Kennedy*. Minneapolis: Twenty-First Century Books, 2004.
John F. Kennedy set the stage for the youth-oriented 1960s. He was assassinated in 1963. This book examines his life, his presidency, and his legacy.

Aronson, Marc. *Up Close: Robert Kennedy*. New York: Viking Juvenile, 2007.
Robert Kennedy worked in his brother John's shadow in the early 1960s. After John's assassination, Robert stepped into the spotlight. Tragically, he too fell to an assassin's bullet. This book tells his story.

Blohm, Craig. *The Great Society: The War on Poverty*. San Diego: Lucent Books, 2004.
Lyndon Johnson's early administration was a time of triumph. He enacted Medicare, Medicaid, Head Start, and other programs as part of his War on Poverty. This book examines these programs and the era that spawned them.

DK Publishing. *Vietnam War*. New York: DK Children, 2005.
This impressive volume uses photographs and fact-filled text to present the grim realities of the war in Vietnam.

Finlayson, Reggie. *We Shall Overcome: The History of the American Civil Rights Movement*. Minneapolis: Twenty-First Century Books, 2003.
Using songs, stories, and other archival material, the author tells the civil rights story from the point of view of those who lived through the movement.

Gourley, Catherine. *Gidgets and Women Warriors: Perceptions of Women in the 1950s and 1960s*. Minneapolis: Twenty-First Century Books, 2008.
This fascinating title examines changing views of women—from the conformist 1950s through the rebellious 1960s. Gourley looks at advertisements, popular magazines, and other media to explore how women of this time were perceived and how they perceived themselves.

Kuhn, Betsy. *The Race for Space: The United States and the Soviet Union Compete for the New Frontier*. Minneapolis: Twenty-First Century Books, 2006.
Using archival photos and historical quotes, Kuhn tells how Americans geared up to beat the Soviets in space. Kuhn follows the race—from *Sputnik* to the moon.

Levy, Debbie. *Lyndon B. Johnson*. Minneapolis: Twenty-First Century Books, 2003.
During his presidency, Lyndon Johnson was much loved and much hated. His Great Society programs were critical to helping lift many Americans out of poverty. Yet Johnson earned much scorn for his handling of the war in Vietnam. This book tells his life story.

———. *The Vietnam War*. Minneapolis: Twenty-First Century Books, 2004.
This title examines the bloody Vietnam conflict in its entirety. Readers will learn about the history of the war, the opposing forces, the home front antiwar movement, and the consequences of war.

Márquez, Herón. *Richard M. Nixon*. Minneapolis: Twenty-First Century Books, 2003.
During the turbulent years of the 1960s, Richard Nixon spoke to those he called "forgotten Americans"—conservative Americans who didn't embrace the counterculture or the antiwar movement. Nixon finally made it to the presidency in 1968, only to fall in disgrace during the Watergate scandal.

Myers, Walter Dean. *The Greatest: Muhammad Ali*. New York: Scholastic Paperbacks, 2001.
As this book shows, Muhammad Ali was more than just a great boxer in the 1960s. He spoke out for Black Power and took a stand against the Vietnam War. This book examines this great sports legend.

Powe-Temperly, Kitty. *The 60s: Mods and Hippies*. Strongsville, OH: Gareth Stevens Publishing, 2000.
Using full-color photos, the author explores the 1960s through fashion. It was a colorful time for clothing, as this book demonstrates.

Roberts, Jeremy. *Bob Dylan: Voice of a Generation*. Minneapolis: Twenty-First Century Books, 2005.
Roberts chronicles Dylan's life, from his boyhood in Minnesota to his folk music years and later rock-and-roll stardom. He also examines the 1960s counterculture that embraced Dylan and his music.

Rubin, Susan Goldman. *Andy Warhol: Pop Art Painter*. New York: Abrams Books for Young Readers, 2006.
The author examines Andy Warhol's life in pictures—his own and the works of those who influenced him. The black-and-white and full-color images bring Warhol's art and work to life.

Spitz, Bob. *Yeah! Yeah! Yeah! The Beatles, Beatlemania, and the Music That Changed the World*. New York: Little, Brown Young Readers, 2007.
This fun-filled book tells the story of the Fab Four—from their roots in Liverpool, England, to world fame. Classic photographs enliven the fascinating text.

Films

Berkeley in the Sixties. DVD. New York: First Run Features, 2002.
This riveting documentary focuses on the University of California at Berkeley in the 1960s. The decade began quietly on campus, but soon Berkeley found itself at the forefront of the antiwar movement.

Bob Dylan: No Direction Home. Directed by Martin Scorsese. DVD. Hollywood, CA: Paramount, 2005.
Here, the award-winning filmmaker Martin Scorsese turns his creative talents to documenting the life and music of Bob Dylan. The film includes insightful interviews with Dylan and others and priceless footage of Dylan both early and later on in his career.

Rebels with a Cause. DVD. New York: Zeitgeist Films, 2003.
This documentary highlights the activities of Students for a Democratic Society, one of the leading and most famous organizations in the fight to end the Vietnam War.

Woodstock: Three Days of Peace and Music. DVD. Burbank, CA: Warner Home Video, 1997.
Those who missed the Woodstock music festival can still experience the crowds, the good vibes, and the music by watching this classic documentary.

Websites

Lyndon Baines Johnson Library and Museum
http://www.lbjlib.utexas.edu/
Lyndon Johnson was a critical part of the upheaval of the 1960s—from the Kennedy assassination to civil rights to the Vietnam War. This website serves as a gateway to Johnson's legacy.

Vietnam Online
http://www.pbs.org/wgbh/amex/vietnam/
This companion site to PBS's *Vietnam: A Television History* offers a wealth of data on the Vietnam War, including a timeline, biographies, and maps.

SELECTED 1960s CLASSICS

Books

Capote, Truman. *In Cold Blood*, 1966. Reprint, New York: Modern Library, 2002.
This "nonfiction novel" tells the brutal true story of murder in a Kansas town in 1959. Capote examines the killers and the victims in intimate detail. The book became an instant classic and is hailed as a masterpiece of New Journalism.

Malcolm X. *The Autobiography of Malcolm X: As Told to Alex Haley*, 1965. Reprint, New York: Ballantine Books, 1992.
Malcolm X urged black Americans to win their freedom "by any means necessary." In this searing autobiography, he tells of his own struggles and spiritual awakening in white-dominated U.S. society. Highly influential when it was first published, the book helped transform the civil rights struggle into a movement for Black Power.

Vonnegut, Kurt. *Slaughterhouse-Five*, 1969. Reprint, New York: Dial Press, 1999.
This darkly comic novel examines the folly of war through the eyes of U.S. soldier Billy Pilgrim. Based on Vonnegut's own experiences in World War II, the book is an antiwar classic and a landmark work of 1960s fiction.

Films

Bonny and Clyde. DVD. Burbank, CA: Warner Home Video, 1999.
This 1967 film faithfully re-creates the Depression-era United States and the exploits of on-the-run criminals Bonnie and Clyde. With its good-looking outlaws and antiestablishment message, the movie struck a nerve with rebellious 1960s audiences.

Dr. Strangelove or: How I Learned to Stop Worrying and Love the Bomb. DVD. Culver City, CA: Sony Pictures, 2001.
Sterling Hayden, George C. Scott, and Peter Sellers star in this hilarious black comedy from director Stanley Kubrick. Will the United States drop nuclear bombs on the Soviet Union? Will the Soviets unleash their own "Doomsday Device" in return? It all sounds serious—but viewers won't stop laughing as they watch this 1964 classic.

The Manchurian Candidate. DVD. Los Angeles: MGM, 2004.
John Frankenheimer's Cold War classic tells a chilling tale of sinister secrets and dark government conspiracies. The 1962 movie stars Laurence Harvey as the troubled Korean War hero Raymond Shaw and Angela Lansbury as his ruthless mother.

1960s ACTIVITY

Identify six to ten things in your own life or family history that relate to the 1960s. (To start you thinking, consider your parents' and grandparents' lives, family antiques or collections, your house or buildings in your neighborhood, favorite movies, books, songs, or TV shows, or places you've visited.) Use photographs, mementos, and words to create a print or computer scrapbook of your 1960s connections.

INDEX

advertisements, 96, 121

African Americans, 37–39, 41, 55, 76–77, 86–87, 125, 129; Black Power, 37–39, 41, 76, 77, 125; musicians, 106–107; segregation, 8–9, 29, 32, 33, 40, 122–123, 129; writers, 76–77

Agent Orange, 19

Aldrin, Buzz, 46

Ali, Muhammad, 117, 118, 119

American Indian Movement (AIM), 42

Angelou, Maya, 76

antinuclear activity, 51, 99, 100, 102

antiwar activity, 19–23, 24–25, 27, 102, 129, 130; religion and, 67

architecture, 80, 88–89, 121; geodesic dome, 80, 89; sports stadiums, 121

Armstrong, Neil, 46

art and design, 81–91

artists: Johns, Jasper, 81–82; Lichtenstein, Roy, 82–83; O'Keeffe, Georgia, 87; Pollock, Jackson, 81; Rauschenberg, Robert, 81, 82; Warhol, Andy, 83, 84–86;

assassinations, 14, 23–24, 26, 36, 39, 41–42, 108, 130

astronauts, 44, 45, 46, 50, 51

atheism, 67

athletes: Ali, Muhammad, 117, 118, 119; King, Billie Jean, 127; Nicklaus, Jack, 120; Palmer, Arnold, 120; Rudolph, Wilma, 116, 117, 127 Starr, Bart, 121–122; Switzer, Kathrine, 126;

baby boomers, 6, 130

Baez, Joan, 34, 108

Baldwin, James, 76, 103

Baraka, Amiri, 76

Bay of Pigs, 12

Beatles, 79, 93, 101, 110–111, 131

Beats, 69, 75

Beatty, Warren, 101

Berrigan brothers, 21, 67

Birmingham, AL, 32–33

birth control, 49, 63, 64

Black Panthers, 38

Black Power, 37–39, 41, 76, 77; at the Olympics, 125

books: *Autobiography of Malcolm X*, 39; *Bell Jar*, 75; *Catch-22*, 74–75; *Feminine Mystique*, 59–60, 79; *In Cold Blood*, 73; *Making of the President*, 70; *On the Road*, 69; *Sex and the Single Girl*, 78–79; *Silent Spring*, 53; *Slaughterhouse Five*, 75; *Steal This* Book, 79; *To Kill a Mockingbird*, 77; *Unsafe at Any Speed*, 52; *Whole Earth Catalog*, 53

Borman, Frank, 47

Boston Marathon, 126

Brautigan, Richard, 74

Brown, Helen Gurley, 78

Brown, James, 38

Cambodia, 27

Campbell's Soup Cans, 84, 85

cancer, 19, 50, 51

Capote, Truman, 73, 85

Carlos, John, 125

Carmichael, Stokely, 37, 38, 39

cars, 6, 48, 52, 91

Carson, Rachel, 53

Cash, Johnny, 114

Castro, Fidel, 12

Chaney, James, 35–36

Chavez, Cesar, 43

Child, Julia, 51

China, 7

civil and equal rights movements, 9, 29–43, 62, 63, 66, 76, 77, 87, 129; music of, 107–109; sports and, 122–124. *See also* feminism

civil rights laws, 15, 26, 32, 34–35, 130

clothing, 22, 63, 89–91, 100, 110, 131

Cold War, 6–7, 12–13, 15, 45, 95

Communism, 6–7, 12, 22; fear of, 7

computers, 48–49

Congress of Racial Equality (CORE), 30, 31, 35–36

Connor, Bull, 32, 33

consumer goods, 6, 8, 48, 50, 52; in art, 84, 91; prices of, 57

counterculture, 63–65, 67, 79, 94–96, 103, 130

Cuban Missile Crisis, 12–13, 26

dance, 106–107, 131

Democratic National Convention (1968), 24–25, 101

Didion, Joan, 78

discrimination, 60, 61, 67, 76

draft (selective service), 20, 21, 22

drugs, 63, 64, 69, 103, 113

Duke, Patty, 100

Dunaway, Faye, 100

Dylan, Bob, 108, 109

earthrise, photo of, 47

education, 20, 56; discrimination in, 8

Eisenhower, Dwight, 4, 5

employment, discrimination in, 8

environmental issues, 51–53, 89, 130

Evers, Medgar, 108

Farmer, James, 30, 31

141

farmworkers, 43

fashion, 22, 63, 89–91, 100

fast foods, 49–50

Federal Bureau of Investigation (FBI), 37, 38

feminism, 49, 59–62, 78–79

food, 49–51, 53; prices of, 57

Freedom Riders, 30–32

Friedan, Betty, 59–60

Fuller, Buckminster, 80, 89

gay issues, 66, 76, 103, 129

generation gap, 64–65

geodesic dome, 80, 89

Ginsberg, Allen, 68, 69, 70, 75

Giovanni, Nikki, 76, 77

Glenn, John, 45, 46

Goldwater, Barry, 15, 96

Gordy, Berry Jr., 106

grape boycott (1965), 43

Great Society, 56

hair, 22, 38, 63, 103, 110, 131

Hair (musical), 103

Halberstam, David, 71

Hamer, Fannie Lou, 35, 36

Haskins, Don, 123

health care, 43, 49, 56

Hendrix, Jimi, 112, 113

Hersh, Seymour, 71

hippies, 63–65, 73, 80, 89, 101, 103; festivals and, 111–113

Hispanic Americans, 42, 43

Hoffman, Abbie, 79

Hoffman, Dustin, 101

Huerta, Dolores, 43

Humphrey, Hubert, 25, 27

ideals, 5–6, 11, 34, 129, 130, 131

"I have a dream" speech, 34

Internet, 48

inventions, 48–49

Jackie O. *See* Kennedy, Jackie (Jackie O)

"jail not bail," 31

Johnson, Lyndon B, 14–15; ads for, 96; social issues, 15, 35, 36, 37, 40–41, 56; Vietnam and, 16, 20, 23, 24

journalism, 70–73

Kennedy, Jackie (Jackie O), 5, 86, 90, 131

Kennedy, John F., 4, 11–15, 26, 45, 67, 90, 130; death of, 14–15, 48, 130; portrait of, 82, on TV, 97

Kennedy, Robert F., 23, 24, 26, 55, 56, 130

Kerner Commission, 40–41

Kerouac, Jack, 69–70

Kesey, Ken, 74

King, Billie Jean, 127

King, Martin Luther, Jr., 9, 23–24, 32–33, 34, 36–37, 67; murder of, 41–42, 130

Kubrick, Stanley, 102

Ku Klux Klan, 36

Lee, Harper, 78

Lennon, John, 79, 110–111

Limited Test Ban Treaty, 51

Lincoln, Abraham, 38

literature, 52, 53, 69–79; poetry, 69, 75, 77; women and, 53, 75, 77–79

magazines and newspapers, 61, 72, 73, 76, 79, 89

Mailer, Norman, 73

Malcolm X, 39, 77

March on Washington, 34

marriage, 59–60, 63, 64

McCarthy, Eugene, 23, 24

McDonald's, 49

McKay, Jim, 119

McLuhan, Marshall, 72

media, 33, 45, 48, 61, 72, 77, 81, 97, 109, 126. *See also* television

miniskirts, 89, 91

Miss America protests, 61

Mississippi Freedom Summer, 35

mod fashion, 89, 91

Monroe, Marilyn, 85

Monterey International Pop Festival, 111, 113

moon landing, 45, 46–47, 131

Morgan, Robin, 79

Motown, 106–107

movies, 86, 98–103, 115; *Bonnie and Clyde*, 101; *Dr. Strangelove*, 99, 102; *Funny Girl*, 115; *Sound of Music*, 99; *2001*, 102; *Valley of the Dolls*, 100

music, 38, 51, 63, 69, 70, 91, 105–115; British Invasion, 109–110; country, 113–114; in film, 101; folk, 34, 51, 108; mainstream, 113–114; Motown, 106–107

music festivals, 111–113

musicians and music groups: Baez, Joan, 34, 108; Beatles, 79, 93, 101, 110–111, 131; Brown, James, 38; Cash, Johnny, 114; Checkers, Chubby, 106; 109; Dylan, Bob, 108, 109; Hendrix, Jimi, 112, 113; Miracles, 107; Presley, Elvis, 9, 93, 105; Shangri-Las, 105, 106; Simon and Garfunkel, 101; Streisand, Barbra, 115

My Lai massacre, 71

142

Nader, Ralph, 52, 130

National Organization for Women (NOW), 62

Native Americans, 42

New Journalism, 72–73

Newton, Huey, 38

New York City, 9, 68, 73, 81, 82, 85, 86–87, 103, 109

Nixon, Richard, 25, 27, 130; on TV, 96, 97

Nixon-Kennedy debates, 97

nonviolence, 9, 30, 37–38, 43

nuclear technology, 7, 9, 12–13, 51, 96; dangers of, 51; opposition to, 51, 99, 100, 102; in pop culture, 96, 99

O'Connor, Flannery, 77–78

O'Hair, Madalyn Murray, 67

O'Keeffe, Georgia, 87

Olympic Games, 117, 118, 119, 125, 127; Black Power at, 125

Oswald, Lee Harvey, 14

patriotism, 9, 11, 22, 65

peace, 11, 21, 64, 65, 67, 96, 112, 129

Peace Corps, 10, 11–12

Plath, Sylvia, 75

poverty, 8, 11, 15, 26, 40, 43, 55; war on, 56

Presley, Elvis, 9, 93, 105

prices, 57

prosperity, 6, 55, 56–57

Quant, Mary, 89, 91

racism, 8–9, 20, 29, 39, 76, 77, 129; in sports, 122–124

Ray, James Earl, 41

religion, 21, 39, 67, 85; Nation of Islam, 39

revolution, 38, 77, 130

Reynolds, Malvina, 51, 53

riots, 25; Stonewall, 66; Watts, 40

Rolling Stone, 79, 109

Rudolph, Wilma, 116, 117, 127

Saarinen, Eero, 88–89

Schwerner, Michael, 35–36

science fiction, 94, 102

Seale, Bobby, 38

segregation, 8–9, 29, 32, 33, 40, 122–123

Selma to Montgomery march, 36–37

Semple, Jack, 126

Sesame Street, 98

sexuality, 42, 49, 64, 76, 78–79, 103, 129; gay rights, 66

Simon and Garfunkel, 101

sit-ins, 28, 29–30, 32

Smith, Tommie, 125

Soviet Union, 7–8, 12–13, 26, 45; limits nuclear testing, 51

space exploration, 7, 45–48, 50–51, 102

sports, 117–127; baseball, 119, 120, 124; basketball, 119, 122–124; boxing, 117, 118; desegregation of, 122–124; football, 120–122; golf, 120, 124; tennis, 124; track, 116, 119, 125; women in, 124, 125–127

Sputnik 1, 7

Starr, Bart, 121, 122

Streisand, Barbra, 114, 115

Student Nonviolent Coordinating Committee (SNCC), 37, 77

Summer of Love, 111

Switzer, Kathrine, 126

TaB, 50

telephones, 49

television, 9, 24, 33, 45, 49, 72, 81, 93–98, 110; sports on, 117, 119, 120

television shows: *Beverly Hillbillies*, 92, 93; *Ed Sullivan Show*, 93, 110; *French Chef*, 51; *Laugh-In*, 95; *Patty Duke Show*, 100; *Sesame Street*, 98; *Star Trek*, 94; *Wide World of Sports*, 117, 119

Tet Offensive, 23, 24

Texas Western, basketball team of, 122–124

theater, 103, 114, 115; *Hair*, 103

Vietnam War, 7, 15–19, 27, 57, 83, 130; massacre in, 71; movement against, 19–23, 63, 64, 70, 73, 102, 128; in popular culture, 67, 70–71, 96, 99, 102, 112, 118; U.S. deaths in, 18, 27, 130

voting rights, 9, 15, 35, 37, 56, 107

Voting Rights Act, 37

Wallace, George, 27, 37, 65

Warhol, Andy, 83, 84–86

War on Poverty, 56

water, 51, 53

Watergate, 130

Westmoreland, William, 23, 24

White, Theodore, 71

Wolfe, Tom, 73–74

women, 6, 42, 49, 69, 77–79; artists, 87–88; clothing and, 89–91; roles of, 6, 20, 58–60, 67, 114, 129; in sports, 124, 126–127; writers, 75, 77–79

Woodstock, 112, 131

work and workers, 8, 41, 43, 56, 56, 60

143

ABOUT THE AUTHOR

Based in California, Edmund Lindop wrote several books for the Presidents Who Dared series as well as several of the titles in The Decades of Twentieth-Century America series.

Margaret J. Goldstein was born in Detroit and graduated from the University of Michigan. She is an editor and author for young readers. She lives in Santa Fe, New Mexico.

PHOTO ACKNOWLEDGMENTS

The images in this book are used with the permission of: © Keystone/Hulton Archive/Getty Images, pp. 3, 131; © MPI/Hulton Archive/Getty Images, pp. 4–5; © Bettmann/CORBIS, pp. 6, 19, 20, 21, 31, 123, 126; Courtesy NSSDC, NASA, p. 7; AP Photo, pp. 8, 10–11, 18, 34, 40, 49, 52, 53, 60, 61, 63, 65, 68–69, 76, 84, 88, 91, 120, 125, 128–129; AP Photo/Museum of Television & Radio/FILE, p. 9; Historical Museum of Southern Florida, p. 13; Library of Congress, pp. 14 (LC-USZ62-134844), 36 (LC-U9-12470B-17), 39 (LC-DIG-ppmsc-01274), 54–55 (LC-USZ62-133299), 140 (left, LC-USZ62-134844); John F. Kennedy Library, p. 15; National Archives, pp. 17 (111-CC-44254), 108 (306-SSM-4C(53)24); © Archive Photos/Hulton Archive/Getty Images, pp. 22–23; AP Photo/Michael Boyer, p. 25; AP Photo/Paul Shane, p. 26; Nixon Presidential Library & Museum, p. 27; © Jack Moebes/CORBIS, pp. 28–29; AP Photo/Bill Hudson, p. 33; © David Fenton/Hulton Archive/Getty Images, p. 38; AP Photo/WX, p. 41; © Joseph Louw/Time & Life Pictures/Getty Images, p. 42; © Arthur Schatz/Time & Life Pictures/Getty Images, p. 43; NASA, pp. 44–45, 46, 47; © SSPL/The Image Works, p. 48; © Pictorial Parade/Hulton Archive/Getty Images, pp. 50, 97; © Bill Eppridge/Time & Life Pictures/Getty Images, p. 56; © H. Armstrong Roberts/Retrofile/Getty Images, pp. 58–59; New York Daily News, p. 66; © Hulton Archive/Getty Images, pp. 70, 112, 140 (right); AP Photo/Horst Faas, p. 71; AP Photo/John Lindsay, p. 72; © Sam Falk/Hulton Archive/Getty Images, p. 73; © Ted Streshinsky/Time & Life Pictures/Getty Images, p. 74; Everett Collection, pp. 75, 95; © Michael Ochs Archives/Getty Images, pp. 77, 104–105; © Ted Streshinsky/CORBIS, p. 78; Cover Photo from the film *How I Won the War*, from *Rolling Stone* November 9, 1967. © Rolling Stone LLC 1967. All Rights Reserved. Reprinted by Permission, p. 79; © Carl Iwasaki/Time & Life Pictures/Getty Images, pp. 80–81; © Burton Berinsky/Time & Life Pictures/Getty Images, p. 82; Art © Estate of Roy Lichtenstein. Photography: Roy Lichtenstein, *Thinking of Him*, 1963, Magna on canvas, 172.7 x 173 cm (68 x 68 1/8 in.), Gift of Richard Brown Baker, B.A. 1935, 1980.29, Yale University Art Gallery/Art Resource, NY, p. 83; © Tony Vaccaro/Hulton Archive/Getty Images, p. 87; © Jim Gray/Hulton Archive/Getty Images, p. 90; © CBS Photo Archive/Hulton Archive/Getty Images, pp. 92–93, 110, 115; Lyndon Baines Johnson Library and Museum, Photo by Democratic National Committee, p. 96; © Sesame Workshop/Courtesy of Everett Collection, p. 98; "THE SOUND OF MUSIC" © 1965 Twentieth Century Fox. All rights reserved. Image courtesy of Everett Collection, p. 99; © FPG/Hulton Archive/Getty Images, p. 100; BONNIE AND CLYDE © Warner Bros.-Seven Arts and Tatira-Hiller Productions. All Rights Reserved. Image courtesy of Everett Collection, p. 101; © Dmitri Kessel/Time & Life Pictures/Getty Images, p. 102; Dezo Hoffman/Rex Features USA, p. 107; © Jill Gibson/Michael Ochs Archives/Getty Images, p. 113; AP Photo/Gene Beley, p. 114; © Mark Kauffman/Time & Life Pictures/Getty Images, pp. 116–117; © Central Press/Hulton Archive/Getty Images, pp. 118, 140 (center); © Art Rickerby/Time & Life Pictures/Getty Images, p. 122; © Dennis Oulds/Central Press/Getty Images, p. 127.

Front Cover: AP Photo/Robert W. Klein (top left); NASA (top right); © Larry Burrows/Time & Life Pictures/Getty Images (bottom left); © Julian Wasser/Time & Life Pictures/Getty Images (bottom right).